Saving our Democracy

Saving Our Democracy

Common Sense
&
Business Strategies

COLIN MAKIN

ISBN: 978-1-945663-99-4

You can always count on the Americans to do the right thing—after they've tried everything else.

Winston S. Churchill

The greatness of America lies in not being more enlightened than any other nation, but rather in her ability to repair her faults.

Alexis de Tocqueville

Contents

Introduction

A couple of important things happened in 2016. We welcomed a new black lab puppy into our home, and there was a Presidential election. Although the two events seemed to be completely unrelated at first, the hours spent getting to know and train our new four-legged friend and the interminable election coverage convinced me that there was actually a very deep connection.

Amidst all the rambunctious and playful behavior, our puppy was showing me that he was trying to learn the basics of how to adapt to his environment and also fit in with acceptable pack behaviors—like not chewing slippers. He appeared very ready to accept authority and conform to the wishes of the pack leaders and even do seemingly pointless things like sitting and lying down when commanded.

The similarities to our election process seemed inescapable. Despite our clear advantage in the area of intellect and our ability to communicate, we were doing more or less what our young dog was doing but in a more sophisticated way. We were getting into groups, actively adapting to the mores of that group and looking for leaders who would support and guide us.

But surely our ability to think sets us apart from the likes of dogs and their wolf ancestors? My research revealed that the answer seems to be a complex mix of "yes" and "no". Yes, we do have a unique capacity to think logically, but it appears that when making social decisions our preset attitudes and basic beliefs oftentimes step in and cut off serious consideration of opposing views and even new information. That would explain much of our current behavior when it comes to what has been described as "tribal" politics. But is that the way it has to be, or is there a way we can replace the current partisan point-scoring squabbles and replace them with productive discussions?

Right now that seems like a remote possibility, but it does not mean we can escape the real-world consequences.

A Wake-up Call

After coming back from working in Canada for a couple of years I was reminded of just how complex and expensive our health care system has become. I came home to incredibly high premiums with eye-watering deductibles, copays, and a bewildering array of restrictions. It had been so much easier north of the border. I was able to get 100% coverage with no deductibles in the same time it took to get my driver's license transferred—in fact, I did both in the same privatized license location at the same time.

But people pay more taxes in Canada, right? True, but that is not entirely the point. Surprisingly enough, the American government is just as generous when it comes to paying for health care through its various agencies like Medicare, Medicaid, Veterans Affairs, and subsidies, etc. If you combine all American governmental expenditures, we actually pay as much per person as a percentage of GDP as Canadians and other Western countries do. In other words, we are already paying the taxes. And to make it worse we are not even getting superior health care—there are many examples of our performance being measurably worse in terms of outcomes. The difference is that we are not getting as much value.

The most obvious victims of an expensive health care system are those who have limited ability to pay. Medicaid helps, but is skimpy and difficult. The working poor avoid preventative care, get sicker, and are in constant fear of the next illness. Entrepreneurs either take the risk of having a high deductible plan or rely on their spouse having decent family coverage. Things aren't much better on the employers' side. Small businesses pay more to insure their employees than big companies, so they find it difficult to attract talent and pay them well. Which means people make employment decisions on the basis of which health plan is best for them rather than where their talents can be best utilized—a colossal misdirection of resources. Most Americans who work for large companies or the government do reasonably well, but even they are finding it necessary to pay more for their portion of the costs. And the problems do not stop there. Even big viable companies find it difficult to support health care costs which forces them to restrain wages and avoid hiring additional staff.

Not only is our health care system complex, difficult, and personally expensive; it also makes our nation less internationally competitive, a fact often overlooked. Regardless of whether you support the provision of health care privately or through the government, it must be recognized that we all pay for our collective health care one way or another. The costs are ultimately supported by our profitable businesses via taxes, payroll deductions, the goods we buy, or as direct payments. How can we expect them to compete when we saddle them with costs that others simply don't have?

So is health care the root of our difficulties when it comes to maintaining our standard of living and international competitive edge? While it is a major factor, our health care system is more of a symptom rather than the disease itself. You would think that our democracy would be able to ensure we get essential services like health care delivered in a cost effective manner if only to protect our economy. But it does not.

Could it be that our system of health care is just an example of how deficient we have become at making fundamentally important decisions for our nation? Have we allowed our government to deteriorate into one run by politicians who are happy to look for arguments to support their ideological preferences and moneyed interests rather than look for practical solutions? It would appear so.

The 2016 presidential election left many confused and concerned for the nation, but others were excited and enthusiastic about the future. Some perceived the election of Donald Trump to be a breath of fresh air; a break from the past with a new leader who would protect us and restore America's greatness. But others saw it as a clear indication that we are not the virtuous example of civilized democracy that we thought we were, and had shown ourselves to be bigoted racists with scant regard for truth and decency. The opposing groups solidified their positions, and the battle lines were drawn.

This book attempts to explain that we have a political system that encourages partisanship, but we citizens are part of the problem. It appears that we still naturally gravitate to the same behaviors that enabled us to survive as a species when we were hunter-gatherers.

Tribal Politics
One primary human behavior is tribalism: meaning to gather into groups of like-minded people and then stick with that group through thick and thin. While tribalism has been a great survival mechanism for many years, it has one very negative aspect when it comes to complex modern societies—we tend to exclusively look for and accept information that supports the opinion of our group. Contrary arguments, even those based in logic or common sense, tend to be ignored.

It is hard to imagine how there could be such a divergence of strongly held views when we all have the same information available to us. It is apparent that careful analysis of candidates' proposals is not the only motivator when it came to voting. Indeed, picking sides on the basis of which group we feel we belong too often seems to be more important. Could it be that humans are not always the logical seekers of truth we think we are?

Can we operate a properly functioning democracy by picking sides and rejecting every idea that appears to offend our group? The answer is probably yes, because we have been doing so for quite some time. But if we do, we will never perform to our full potential. We have spent too much time and energy playing partisan politics and chasing short-term easy fixes. The stakes are high and getting higher—if we don't come to grips with the real issues, we will become steadily less competitive and suffer the inevitable consequences.

Politics as Usual
So what do we do now? Surely we can't go on having our nation driven by emotions based on the same instincts we needed to survive when our forebears were competing with wolves for food. However, even if we want to, we cannot simply jettison our emotions and act like Dr. Spock. Good or bad, we are human and always will be. The answer must be to embrace the fact that we are Homo Sapiens and enjoy the freedom to have different feelings and opinions; but also be able to recognize and embrace our common goals and then use logic to plot a course for the betterment of all.

A Common Sense Solution
If we accept the fact that our political system performs poorly because it lacks a framework that demands clear thinking and honesty, simple logic suggests that we incorporate structures that we know work in other areas of our life. Fortunately, we don't have to look far.

We have been able to fashion social mechanisms that keep our behavioral instincts in check by forcing us to act logically. Examples include science and technology because both require rational thought and repeatable results. Another example is how we operate business, particularly in a free market economy because unlike politics it requires the truth at all times and demands results in a cost-effective manner. The last few chapters of the book provide suggestions on how we can encourage and then incorporate a number of sound business practices into our political system, thereby making it operate in a data-driven, results-based manner—just like we do in the commercial world.

The first step is not to blame others, but to take a good hard look in the mirror and ask ourselves why we allow, and perhaps, even encourage tribal politics to rule our lives. Unchallenged group-think has never worked in science, technology or business—why would it work in politics?

Can we change our political system to operate using objective truth and logic just like our scientific, technical and commercial worlds do? The answer is yes, but it will not be easy. If we do succeed, however, we will develop a better functioning democracy and a more competitive and wealthier nation.

Colin Makin
March, 2019

Chapter 1

What My Dog Taught Me

If you understand dogs, you understand most human behavior

Have you ever wondered why we get along with dogs so well? On the surface, it seems like an unlikely relationship, particularly when you remember that all dogs are descendants of wolves. How could a carnivorous pack animal swap sides and join with a competing species? Surely it would be a dangerous and untenable situation for both sides. It turns out that the brainier of the two species actually found uses for the wolf and just as importantly the wolf found a use for humans. Like all successful long-term relationships, there had to be mutual benefit, but it required work and accommodation on both sides. It took many years to develop breeds with desired traits, but it eventually resulted in the various sizes, shapes, and capabilities that we see today.

Even after all that genetic manipulation our friends have not lost their essential doggieness—part of which is their innate desire to be part of the pack. And we humans have not lost our need to be part of a pack either. Could it be that the essentials of pack life, whether dog or human, are so similar that the rules are much the same? If that is true, there is likely much we can learn about ourselves from studying our canine companions.

Owning dogs is a popular thing, but it doesn't seem to make a lot of sense. They are expensive to buy, feed, house, and keep healthy. They take a lot of time to train, chew valuable items, make messes, shed hair, and render any sort of social event or travel plan much more difficult. All in all, they need a heck of a lot of looking after. It's a long list of negatives, so the positives must be extremely significant because almost 40% of American households have dogs. Some people own dogs because they are useful. Service, hunting, and sheep herding dogs come to mind, but that is clearly a minority. In short, the appeal of dogs cannot be based on logic or even what you might call common sense. It is my belief that dogs develop a very special bond with humans because they are simplistic reflections of what we see as the friendly, good and loyal, or at least the uncomplicated, side of ourselves. Even when they try to be manipulative it is so obvious that we see it as a fun part of their personality. The fact is, we have so many similar traits that our canine companions start to feel like a member of the family.

Why would a hairy creature with sharp teeth, an exceptional sense of smell, and no ability to speak have characteristics similar to our own? The answer is that our social brains are similar because both species learned parallel survival skills during our early stages of development. Most importantly, the skill of how to survive as pack/tribal animals. Since they found a successful strategy for survival, wolves have stayed pretty much the same for the last million years, whereas humans took the route of evolving bigger brains. We did not, however, lose our core survival techniques, including the development and maintenance of a functioning social hierarchy.

So here we are, two species, each crafted by evolution to hunt utilizing the winning strategies of cooperation and communal living. Both humans and dogs have a basic motivation to establish a tribe or pack based on the need for social order. By happy coincidence our concept of what functions as a workable hierarchy seems to coincide quite well with that of dogs, and we can communicate well enough to make a blended pack within which dogs and humans seem to know their rightful places in the chain of command. Having humans as leaders of the pack makes the most sense for everyone—after all, it is the humans who provide the basics, like food and shelter, for survival. But no one-sided arrangement lasts for very long, so it makes sense that our canine friends really do provide something to offset all of the downsides. President Harry Truman is reported to have said, "If you want a friend in Washington, get a dog." Whether the quotation is true or not, I think it underlines the essence of why dogs have remained popular companions for so long. As well as having useful functions, like being a guard dog, they have also provided much more for thousands of years. Evidence of this is seen in the archeological record that shows dogs were nursed through serious illnesses and even given a proper burial. They continue to provide companionship which is unencumbered by morality, agenda, deception, hidden alliances, and beliefs. It is a simple and honest friendship.

It appears to me that we can learn a lot from this special relationship because in a social sense dogs are very much like we were when we first started to walk on two legs but before we developed our massive and complicated brains. Indeed, you could be forgiven for thinking that a thorough understanding of dogs could lead to a good explanation for much of all human social behavior. For example, both humans and dogs operate at their best when they feel secure. They need to understand how they fit into their own group, who is in charge, and how they are expected to behave with not only their peers but also pack members throughout the social hierarchy. They also have to feel useful—both dogs and humans like to be productive and be recognized for their contributions. On the other hand, both dogs and humans that feel unappreciated or are unsure of who is in charge and what is expected of them can act out their social insecurity in all sorts of seemingly unpredictable and undesirable ways. Does that sound like anyone you know?

Lessons from Kirkby and Kendal
We brought our new black Lab puppy home when he was just six weeks old. Right from the start Kendal was a great deal of work, but also a lot of fun. While we mostly knew what to expect there were a few surprises. In many respects he acted just like Kirkby, the previous Lab we had many years ago, but in certain respects he was very different.

Kirkby had what might be described as a nervous disposition, or rather the good sense to back away from scary or uncomfortable things. Our new canine companion was showing very early signs of being quite different. Some uncomfortable or even painful things were not to be avoided—they were to be responded to in kind. A thistle that pricked his mouth could not be allowed to get away with it. He would take a step back, lunge, and bite it again, only to repeat the process because the thistle obviously wanted to fight. The noise of vacuum cleaners is an annoyance to many dogs and neither of ours were an exception. While Kirkby would take a hike to the next room and often shut the door behind himself, Kendal would attack the vacuum cleaner until it gave up trying to challenge him by submitting and switching itself off. Although the same breed, Kirkby and Kendal had very different outlooks on life much like humans of differing political persuasions.

That's not to say that Kendal could not sense danger. Many new things would elicit suspicion or even fear. The first car that drove by was a very scary thing, the next one less so, and now the only ones noticed are those with loud exhausts and others having the desire to share rap music with the world.

Actions resulting in pleasure required a learning curve too—but not a long one. Getting to successfully associate a command to "sit" and "stay" with food treats had very short learning curves. And just one rewarding interaction with a friendly human or dog in the neighborhood would cause barely controllable urges to run across the street to reinforce the relationship on every subsequent encounter.

All of Kendal's behaviors were definitely well within the scope of those that can reasonably be expected of dogs, but they also seemed to have parallels and even similarities to those of humans. His desire for comfort, affection, and reassurance seemed to be very similar to the wants of young children and even adults. But then he would do things that were not very human-like. Sniffing the ground where another dog had urinated, eating deer poop, and rolling in decaying carcasses are things that we humans just don't do. We do, however, have our own versions—we have Facebook, eat some strange stuff, and like to smell nice.

So what are we to make of these similarities and differences between dogs and humans, and how does that help us understand ourselves and make our lives better?

Genetics
I think that the very fact that we can stand back, identify a dog's actions, and say "but of course, it's a dog" helps us clarify what really brought about a particular behavior. When a dog is affectionate, runs fast, swims, retrieves, or is adept at herding sheep we can usually attribute a trait to a particular breed. But they all have generalized wolf-based dog traits together with their own breed and individual characteristics. The character and abilities that dogs are born with are collectively dictated by their wolf ancestry, breed, family tree, and the unique genetic message that make an individual dog different from all others on the planet.

The same rules apply to us except that dogs are artificial animals —all of them descendants of wolves and genetically engineered by humans through continuous selective breeding so that they finally exhibited desired sizes, shapes, and behaviors. Humans are closer to the wolf model because we have stayed much the same as we were when the first Homo Sapiens appeared. No outside force other than nature has intervened to direct our genetics. Therefore, we humans, apart from familial and personal differences, are now all pretty much the same. In a very basic sense, we are all pre-set to react and behave in very similar ways without coming close to having to consciously think.

Education and Experiences
Wolves have a natural proclivity to fit in and be part of a hierarchical pack and their dog descendants have not lost that imperative, which is why they can fit easily and naturally into our human family structure. This is particularly true if they are

trained to be subordinate to the two-legged members of the "pack."

When a dog is responsive to commands and generally behaves well it is almost always attributed to the training the dog received when growing up. That is the formal side of the dog's education, but of course that is not the complete educational experience. Unfortunate or traumatic experiences such as cruelty, neglect, or accidents can have profound and permanent effects on a dog. Our first dog, Kirkby, must have had an unfortunate experience with a slippery floor when he was young because any kind of shiny surface like tiles and ice were a no-go his entire life. By the same token, pleasurable interactions can help mold a dog into one that is secure without debilitating fears and anxieties.

You would think that fear and insecurity might cause dogs to seek safety. But that is not always the case. They very often exhibit aggression if they are unsure of their owner's capabilities, authority, or intent. If they cannot rely on their owner to take a leadership role they sometimes become unsure of themselves and how to act, particularly if something different or unusual occurs. Without appropriate mentorship humans are no different. Early formative experiences have a tendency to affect people's behaviors throughout their lives. Children who live in loving and caring homes are likely to build similar environments when they grow up, but young boys raised in an abusive home very often repeat that behavior without being fully aware of why. Even in adulthood repeated messages and experiences can become ingrained in a person's psyche, particularly if it is experienced communally with others in the same group.

Circumstances
When he was about three months old Kendal started to react to new sounds coming from outside of the house. He appeared to be taking on the responsibility of being the guard dog, barking, and looking out of the front window to see what was going on. It was all a bit irritating, but he was obviously "being a dog". Deep in his brain there was an instruction to warn the pack that there

was potential danger. We will get him out of the habit eventually as he learns that there really is no danger out there and that barking annoys the bipedal leaders of the pack.

Well, that's what happened when our first dog, Kirkby, was growing up. For the most part he was a well-adjusted dog (apart from the slippery floor problem) and he just didn't have too many excessive fears. But one night we were out walking in a wooded area close to our home and we heard a coyote howl and it seemed fairly close. Our immediate reactions were pretty similar — "what the heck was that?" My initial feelings quickly gave way to the rational explanation of the noise and the understanding that the possibility of a coyote attack was extremely remote. It was a different experience for Kirkby. The combination of the very dark night and the howl of a hungry carnivore produced a reaction that came as a big surprise to me. Instead of investigating or just walking and sniffing at the end of a fairly long leash, he immediately came back as close to me as he could. And he remained that way until we got out of the unlit wooded area. What had just happened?

When he had previously heard coyotes Kirkby would definitely take note, but would not react with fear for the simple reason that he was in the house and safe. The night walk in the woods was different because of the lack of visibility and exposure to the potential dangers lurking in the trees clearly made a big difference. His reaction was clearly brought on by the circumstances, which brought about insecurity. It was immediate, visceral, and driven by an survival instincts.

No animal would survive unless it had a built-in desire to eat and wolves are no exception. They are constantly on the lookout for food sources in its various forms, but the way they go about it is affected by circumstance. A wolf that has just eaten will likely turn its nose up at the prospect of hunting if a great deal of effort is required. However, hunger changes things completely, and a wolf would even expose itself to injury if it is close to starving. Survival requires wolves be primed to react to a multitude of other challenges including the universal instantaneous response to danger known as "fight or flight", and unsurprisingly dogs are no different. The genetics and character of a particular animal might dictate that it is predisposed to aggression or self-preservation, but the actual response will be affected by specific circumstances. Meeting people on walking trails near our home is a pleasurable experience for Kendal and it usually elicits energetic tail wagging and the desire to sniff or lick, but a jogger coming up quickly from behind changes things completely. Unlike slow-moving humans walking towards us, the jogger is perceived to be a clear and present danger The resulting aggressive barking does not come from intellectual considerations, it comes from deeply embedded survival instincts. Fast-moving humans coming from behind brings about immediate and intense feelings of insecurity. It is clear that meeting humans for the first time can cause pleasure or fear—it largely depends on the circumstances of the meeting.

Conclusions

After analyzing our dogs' behaviors I came to the conclusion that they were brought about by a combination of only three factors:

- Genetics: canine, breed, and individual
- Experience: formative experiences, formal and informal training
- Circumstance: environment, security (physical and emotional)

A more uncomfortable conclusion was that human thoughts and behaviors are subject to those same variables. Not only that, it would appear that a part of the human brain functions the same way as a dog's, as evidenced by our similar responses to external stimuli like danger and our ability and overpowering desire to establish and maintain socially cohesive groups. But that is where the similarities end. We have been imbued with much more sophisticated social skills and an ability to think logically. It is as though we have two brains, one emotional and the other logical. Just to make it all the more confusing, it appears that they are able to communicate with each other but can also operate independently without us being totally aware of it.

It should be noted that all of the uniquely human functions made possible by our big logical brains were <u>added</u> to our already formed basic survival and socially driven brains. They did not replace them. Our emotional brain handles immediate issues and tries to confirm that what we are seeing and hearing conforms to a pattern of understanding that has already been established by previous learning. Only when something really strange or difficult happens does the issue get passed onto the logical brain. Clearly there is a preference to keep things simple and just get on with things, which in most cases gets us through life in the most efficient way. But getting through life on auto-pilot which has been programmed by preconceived notions presents us with a very human problem. It would appear that we can't stop ourselves from being human any more than dogs can stop themselves from being dogs.

In a sense, dogs are lucky. They can survive relying entirely on the basis of predetermined reactions based on hard-wired emotions and learned responses—all they have to do is get on with their lives without any thought of whether or not their actions have long-term ramifications. It is different for us because most of our uniqueness and success as a species has come from our ability to think logically and then pass on knowledge to the next generation. The trouble is that in certain parts of our lives, notably the political world, we find it very difficult to separate emotional and logical thought. The unfortunate effect is that we reward politicians who have the greatest emotional appeal and then entrust them with tasks requiring the use of logic, like the management of our government. Is it any wonder there is a lack of focus on real issues and that performance plays second fiddle to rhetoric? Democracy can be very frustrating.

Other nations unencumbered by the messy business of operating a democracy find it much easier to identify long-term issues and execute appropriate plans because they do not have to play games with the emotions of their electorate. China is particularly adept at putting together pragmatic plans and then executing them competently, as evidenced by their massive infrastructure projects and clear headed focus on science and industries of the future They are showing us the power of logical thought and competent execution. We are obviously not going to adopt China's authoritarian one-party system of government, so the question becomes: can we re-engineer our political system so that we get the best of both worlds? The freedom inherent with democracy but also take advantage of our human ability to think logically rather than our tendency to react with our pre-set emotions?

If we can't we will become less and less able to compete and maintain living standards.

Chapter 2

The Trump Phenomenon

The election of Donald Trump as President of the United States uniquely underscored the strengths and weaknesses of our democracy.

A Big Surprise

On November 9th, 2016 I was not alone—like many people across this country, I asked myself why Donald Trump had been elected president of the United States of America. It was certainly a big surprise, but in retrospect it was not completely out of the blue. During the Republican primary it gradually became evident that he had been able to uncover something deep inside the minds of many Republican voters that most political pundits and lay people alike didn't even know was there. Then it gradually dawned on pollsters that he had connected with not only Republicans but also many Democrats and independents. Although unable to win the popular vote, he was able to garner enough support to be elected president via the electoral college. Members of both conservative and liberal establishments could only look on in disbelief. It was a major upset, to say the least.

Clearly, some introspection was in order and all sorts of theories have been put forward. Many of them, like the conclusion that we must be a nation of racists or too stupid and ill-informed to understand the implications of a Trump presidency just don't pass muster. Many of us know Trump supporters and by and large they are far from stupid, are reasonably well-informed, and not racist in the traditional sense of the word. That is not to say that there was not a dark side to some of his support—as evidenced by the ultra-right and white nationalists who gradually came out of the woodwork and showed themselves to to be aligned with some of the not so subtle "dog whistles." Sure, they are mainly older white guys who prefer to socialize with others who come from more or less the same backgrounds and have had similar life experiences but that does not make them racist. What primarily holds them together is the conservative view that if you want to improve your lot in life you must work hard and play by the rules and since America offers everyone opportunities to succeed it's simply up to you. Further, no one should be cosseted or rewarded for adopting poor life strategies. It is a group that will never buy into anything that looks like a socialist agenda, and there are a lot of them—basically, committed Republicans.

You can certainly see why traditional Republican supporters would reject Hilary Clinton's prescription for improving America, but a belief in conservative principles does not explain how or why Trump secured the Republican nomination. So what was Trump offering that others in the GOP were not? And what made enough Democrats switch sides?

If we are to understand and learn from the election of Donald J. Trump we must answer some pretty perplexing questions:

- Why would someone advocating tax reductions along with massive spending and no corresponding budget cuts become the Republican nominee, particularly when the Tea Party had recently become such a powerful influence?
- Why did evangelical Christians prefer this thrice married, philandering, woman abuser who professed to share their faith (but no one really believed) become the preferred choice over better-behaved (and apparently) genuine Christians?
- How could someone with scant knowledge of domestic and foreign policy issues gain the trust of voters?
- Why did proposals appealing to religious bigotry and others with clear racist overtones not attract sufficient opposition to make this candidate unacceptable?

Donald Trump could not have been elected on the basis of fulfilling all of the standard political requirements like: sticking with the party platform, message discipline, having semi-plausible policy proposals, and resisting the temptation to offend. So why was the American public prepared to take a chance on this man? What he was offering must have been HUGE. And it was.

Insecurity and Leadership

If a politician wants to evoke strong emotions it is always a good idea to play to insecurities and Donald Trump did a masterful job of playing to a number of them. But before he even got to that point he developed an image of being a strong leader. After all, what good is a politician who points out that you are in danger if he is incapable of saving you from it? Hosting a reality TV show that depicted him as decisive and powerful, able and willing to flaunt wealth, and then denigrating any and all competitors with blunt and aggressive language illustrated to many voters that he could be an effective protector. There were a number of aspects to the insecurity pitch.

The message that the current and recent administrations were incompetent, corrupt, and incapable of looking after the nation resonated with our basic human need for strong leadership. After all, our weak and incompetent government and elites had allowed the financial crash to destroy the economy, ignored defense, and hurt the middle class by agreeing to unfair trade deals. They also made a mess of health care and allowed our allies to get subsidized protection since we paid for their defense.

Beyond the more traditional policy issues, Trump also drummed up cultural fears. The threat of Mexican "hoards" bringing drugs and crime clearly struck a chord with the hard-wired instinct we all have to fear strangers that are coming to harm us. Images of Muslims cheering on 9/11 and hyperbole regarding Sharia law were advanced to show that these people were intent on creating their own society within our country.

An appeal to patriotism can be very effective, especially if you can convince the public that they are defenseless and under attack. Therefore, the concept that we were being taken advantage of had an audience that had been primed by the Obama presidency. Obama was seen by many as a leader with a long list of actions that demonstrated a perceived weakness and supposed disdain for America, including: apologizing for America on overseas trips, setting red lines and then retreating, allowing terrorists to kill Americans in Benghazi, allowing the military to atrophy, etc. In addition to failing to respond to physical threats, Obama also failed to protect American workers from unfair foreign competition.

Obama was also seen as weak when it came to simply getting things to work. Although a powerful speaker, he seemed incapable of getting the government to function properly. Who better to look after us than a strong, hard-driving, deal-making businessman who could break all the rules, get things moving, and ensure we wouldn't be kicked around anymore?

The trouble with those arguing against Donald Trump was that he had a message that went straight to some of our deepest emotions. And it was supported by the logical argument that he had business credentials so he would be able to cut through the Washington dysfunction and make things work. There also weren't that many good alternatives. No other candidate in the Republican field came prepared to win on the basis of projecting greater strength. All they had to offer was a traditional Republican approach and a "trust me" disposition. Well, we had tried that before, which was the same problem for any Democrat —and we had certainly done the Clinton thing before.

The Political Sales Process

Although Donald Trump had a message and the personality to sell it, no one should think what he achieved was easy or inevitable. Like all complex sales campaigns it required a focused and disciplined execution.

Step 1: The Approach

The first step is known as the "approach". It acts as an introduction by giving the prospective customer an opportunity to get an idea of who you are as a person, rather than just a vendor. Trump did this by being the star of a reality TV show and it would prove to be invaluable in the later stages of his campaign. He became known to millions of people and was widely perceived to be a proactive, decisive, and potentially ruthless person who could get things done. Someone who you would like to have on your side. The persona was reinforced during the "Birther" stage of the approach. In addition to being seen as tough, he could now be seen as wanting to stand up for a disappearing America in which only "real" Americans got to be president.

Step 2: The Conversion

After the approach has been successfully undertaken it is necessary to change a potential customer into a paying one, or in the political world the electorate into voters. The process is one of motivation and includes establishing dissatisfaction with the current product followed up with the promise of a better future.

a) Dissatisfaction   There were obviously fertile grounds to sow the seeds of dissatisfaction. Any reasonable person need only look at all that had gone wrong in recent years, both internationally and domestically, to develop a long list of problems. The continual decline of middle-class living standards made so much worse by the 2008 financial crisis and subsequent slow recovery, military quagmires in the Middle East, terrorist actions at home and abroad, and the apparent continual unchallenged waves of illegal immigration. It all combined to create a feeling that the country was headed in the wrong direction. From a sales process point of view, Trump did exactly the right thing—he validated peoples' feelings of dissatisfaction in a way that they felt heard. To make sure everyone got the point he threw in hyperbole to make things appear even worse than people had originally felt. He then went on to emphasize that the current service provider—"the elites", supported by the established political party industry—was either incapable or unwilling to put things right.

Next, it was necessary to get on board with all of the other Republicans and reinforce the message that the Democrats were intent on ruining the country with their socialistic, anti-business, anti-gun, immigrant-loving, un-Christian, pro-abortion policies. He shook off most of his previous left-wing ideas and became a bona fide Republican. Then he needed a way to differentiate himself from the rest of the candidates in the Republican primary and point out why Republicans should be dissatisfied with their existing party. In the process he proved that not only the rank and file, but also the majority of the party faithful did not want a return to the traditional official, implied, and perceived messages:

- What is good for business is good for you, trust me
- If we give the wealthy enough money, they will become the job creators
- Social Security, Medicaid, and Medicare are luxuries we cannot afford
- Spend whatever it takes to protect allied nations
- Spend money and resources to make other countries more like us and if necessary, bomb and invade
- Feeding fat cat elites and special interests living off of the government is acceptable, so long as they donate to the party
- Immigration control just requires lip service
- Imports from countries that restrict our exports are okay if it keeps costs down
- Profess support for small business but do the bidding of big companies

During the Republican primary it became a choice between a fresh but somewhat scary face and the same old tired Republicans trying hard to conform to whatever they saw as the checklist of acceptability. We had seen it all before.

The country was ready for a change and Trump knew he was onto a winner with his populist anti-establishment message, but it was obvious that he couldn't win if he retained too many of the left-leaning views he had held for many years. Good sense dictated he would have to become a staunch defender of the Second Amendment, the unborn, right-wing judges, and Christianity, etc. With all of the major right-wing social single-issue voters on board and a snappy populist message he looked good for the primary. In doing so, Trump proved himself to be more politically astute than the ideologically driven conservatives in the party. He recognized he was not talking to anyone's elites—be they Left or Right—he was talking to the average guy. As far as Trump was concerned the elites and party grandees in the Republican Party were just as out of touch as those on the left. Talking in an unusually blunt manner without the standard political dodging and weaving was a tremendous plus when it came to messaging. But it was not just the style of delivery, he proposed simple and strong solutions to the economy, illegal immigration, and threats of terrorism. He also recognized that in the real world, it is not just Democrats who are motivated to keep government programs like Social Security, Medicare, and Medicaid—rank and file Republicans depend on them too.

Trump, therefore, had the complete message for the man in the street who had been feeling insecure for years. Well-paying jobs would return along with the respect that comes along with doing useful work because trade would be made fairer; immigrants would not be able to take jobs or threaten us culturally and physically; health care would be better and more affordable; our military would be stronger; essential social programs would be protected; taxes would be reduced; and the deficit would disappear because economic growth would pay for any shortfall. Lastly, we would get back to doing things like we used to before we were pushed around by foreigners and our national prestige would be restored.

The Trump message was primarily aimed at Republicans so there was serious doubt that it would resonate with enough Democrats and independents to win the general election. Surely his negative image amongst minorities, women, and even Conservatives would be sufficient enough to doom his candidacy when added to a horrified and motivated Democratic base? It was not for two very good reasons.

First, it turns out that many of the voters Democrats had relied upon in the past were just as fed up with their party as the majority of Republicans were of theirs. They did not want a continuation of the perceived traditional Democratic approaches:

- Increase regulations that stifle economic and job growth
- Encourage immigrants whose cultures will overwhelm ours
- Encourage undocumented immigrants to become citizens
- Support of unions and government workers
- Pander to anyone with a sense of grievance
- Have disdain for traditional American values
- Have a weak-kneed foreign policy
- Allow the erosion of American power
- Allow high health care premiums
- Talk the talk but lack a plan to improve job opportunities
- Deference to all cultures but our own and encourage hyper-political correctness
- Feeding fat cat elites and special interest groups living off of the government is acceptable, so long as they donate to the party
- Acceptance of lazy people living off of the government
- Installing left-leaning judges represents progress
- Putting climate control ahead of jobs
- Excessive government spending
- Being stridently pro-choice

Second, the Democrats had a problem candidate. Although Trump looked pretty scary, many saw Hillary Clinton as an even bigger gamble. A continuation of the Clinton dynasty just did not have much appeal. In many peoples' minds, it would be a continuation of Obama's slow growth, but also with a return to sleazy behaviors perfected by the Clintons in the 90s. The use of a private server created suspicion—supported by the FBI—that she was up to something, or at least playing fast and loose with national secrets, worried a lot of people. Hillary Clinton appeared to be:

- A self-serving politician who became wealthy through connections and pay-to-play politics.
- Someone who would put personal secrecy and convenience above national security.
- A politician who would always be above the law.
- Someone who could simply not be trusted to tell the truth.
- A candidate who lacked a clear plan that would put America back on the right track.

In short, voters rejected the idea that the same people in both parties who had presided over stagnant middle-class wages since the 70s, got us into wars in the Middle East, and then led us all into the 2008 financial crisis could be relied upon to put things right in the future. Continuing to depend on those experts and elites who drove the bus off the road—but who all came back out of the ditch smelling like roses—just didn't seem to make sense. The old order was well past its sell-by date. Something new was worth a try, and there is nothing illogical about that. In a sense, Trump had an easy job of stoking dissatisfaction with both parties and he did so in a unique and masterful manner.

b) Future Promise Of course, telling potential customers that they have a problem is only the first step. The successful salesperson then has to convince the potential customer that they have a unique and workable proposition. Like all good sales operations Trump's selling strategy was very simple. He gave direct sound-bite solutions to problems and then presented a plausible reason to believe he could implement the necessary changes. Through his appearances on reality TV he had shown himself to be a powerful person who was able to act decisively and make things happen. The type of person you would want on your side. He was a proven negotiator who had accomplished real estate deals worldwide. Who could argue with his capabilities? After all, he was a billionaire and had surpassed the entire field of professional politicians during the Republican primary. Who would you want fighting for you, a failed venal politician or a successful businessman who could get to the essence of a problem and hire the right people to make it all work?

For many people, making a big change made sense. However, even though he could project an image of strength, the candidacy of Donald Trump presented some real problems when it came to the general election. If America were a company looking for a new CEO or president, they would not be looking for a pure salesman. They would be looking for someone with proven high-level executive experience, so he would probably not have gotten past an HR review of his resume. If he did get to the interview stage the lack of experience and many of his pronouncements would likely cause major problems. The treatment of women, cozying up to Russia, and having no workable and/or coherent strategies would just not be in alignment with the job description. And one could imagine that the multiple-choice aptitude test would expose some real character issues. Even if HR were to give him a pass with reservations, surely the board of directors would give him the thumbs down. Human Resources and the board would have a point—there were a thousand and one reasons not to vote for him. Even many of his supporters saw him as a thin-skinned narcissist with a short attention span and highly questionable management skills. Something of a boorish lout with a very loose attachment to the truth. And who wants a loose cannon in charge of our nuclear arsenal?

Step 3: Buying Motivations
Clearly there was some serious work to be done to get elected. After establishing the feeling dissatisfaction and validating the vision of a better future, the sales operation must communicate more specifics to ensure that the buying motives of the customer are identified and addressed. Most sales professionals accept that while there are few buying motivations, they are definable and the more you can recognize and satisfy the greater likelihood of

success. This is particularly true if the product is intended for a mass market. Trump achieved this in the following manner:

1. *Security.* In a social sense, loss of security often results in the powerful emotion of fear, so it made sense for the Trump campaign to emphasize current and future dangers. Immigrants from Mexico were not just crossing the border in numbers never seen before, a large percentage were rapists, murderers, and drug dealers. Muslims entering the country had no intention of assimilating and were actively creating no-go areas for Christians and the police, and to make it worse they were supporters of terrorist acts. Further, our military had become so degraded that we were being bullied and were unable to defend ourselves. In short, the message was that Americans should be scared because it's bad and only getting worse.

   Along with all of the dangers originating from outside of the country, there were also home-grown threats. Large areas of American cities were war zones where it was unsafe to walk because minorities were shooting each other. And there were more than just physical threats. Due to ineffective and corrupt political leadership, the financial situations and job prospects of many Americans were in jeopardy due to multiple bad trade deals our politicians had made over the years. A strong leader from outside of the current political "swamp" in Washington with a proven record of getting things done was necessary.

2. *Pride and Prestige.* Even before the Declaration of Independence, Americans believed they were creating something very special. The concept of American exceptionalism was born out of a feeling that the country stood out from all other nations, not to be judged in terms of brute power alone, but on ideals.

America's reliance on the fundamentals of fairness, democracy, the rule of law, and free enterprise was a bold experiment, but it resulted in a country that was strong enough to protect and guide the world through an extended period of peace and prosperity. Quite an achievement for a collection of English colonies on the east coast of North America—it is small wonder that American hearts swell with pride and feelings of patriotism. While all politicians play the patriotism card, Trump did it more effectively than most because he presented himself as the only candidate strong enough to make it happen. The "Make America Great Again" slogan worked on two very important human emotions. Patriotism was first and most obvious, but it also very successfully appealed to the sense of loss. The promise of restoring power and prestige to the nation proved to be just what much of the country was looking for.

3. *Affiliation*. In the commercial world, affiliation refers to a desire to be a part of a group and feel at one with their wants and purpose—like millions of Apple, Google, and Amazon customers all over the world. In a political sense, the biggest group we belong to is the human race, but most of us only start to feel part of a real group when we consider ourselves to be part of an ethnic group or a citizen of a nation. For thousands of years people have been willing to suffer unimaginable privations, give up everything, and fight and die for their tribe or country. The desire to preserve and protect your own group has always been one of the strongest of all human emotions.

Trump's appeal to "Make America Great Again" was a particularly effective message because it solidified groups who felt ongoing changes in society were undermining the very foundations of what made

America great in the first place. It was a promise to restore what had been lost.

And what was lost? The answer to that was practically anything you wanted it to be: for older white males, it could be a loss of relative status; for factory workers, good living wages; for patriots, American prestige; for Christians, their universally held beliefs and behaviors —the list goes on. Just about everyone had something on the list of losses that they could relate to, but the message had particular appeal to older white males without a college education. For them there really was a bygone age when everything was better, so it is unsurprising that they formed a solid base for Trump's support.

The opposition then unwittingly solidified those groups by failing to understand another human emotional driver—when members of a group are attacked they bond even more tightly. Democrats made them all the more committed by writing them off as uneducated bigots who were in large part "deplorable," and even "irredeemable." And then after the election we saw group cohesion on both sides further solidify during the confirmation hearings of Justice Brett Kavanaugh. The appointment of conservative judges was seen by many as the biggest single way to ensure society would not slide into being controlled by progressive elites, so having both chambers and the presidency became even more important than searching for a perfect president. As long as he is "our" president, that's good enough.

4. *Profit or Gain.* There are a number of single-issue voter groups that will never support a politician who does not stand with them on their own personal and deeply held beliefs. The anti-abortion, Second Amendment and anti-gay marriage proponents come

to mind. Although significant, these groups are not the biggest. In normal peacetime situations the most significant single-issue voting group is the one that believes in a strong economy. This is not just money in a venal or accounting sense. It is an emotional and deeply held view that the economy is the lifeblood of the nation—without it personal aspiration and freedom would die. Trump quite rightly appealed to the nation's belief that personal freedom only exists in a properly functioning economy. His message not only promised an escape from the drudgery of a poor economy, but also the stultifying effects of having to rely on the whim of a corrupt and incompetent government. Of course every politician promises the same, but a direct proposition from someone who had seemingly proven himself to be successful in the business world just had more credibility than career politicians. The Trump message simply felt better.

5. *Avoidance of Pain.* Only rarely do politicians call on their electorate to accept additional burdens. During his inaugural speech JFK proclaimed, "Ask not what your country can do for you, ask what you can do for your country," but that sort of call for personal duty and sacrifice has now largely fallen out of favor. The modern and most successful approach is to propose solutions that take pain away from just about everyone. For example, during the Iraq war the biggest sacrifice non-military citizens had to take was to keep shopping. And from a pain-avoidance perspective, Trump's message was every bit as good. Taxes would be drastically reduced, health care would improve in quality and affordability, essential programs like Social Security, Medicare, and Medicaid would be untouched, the deficit would disappear, and everyone who wanted a job would get one and it

would pay more. This was clearly superior to anything the established parties were offering.

6. *Comfort/Pleasure.* The Trump message was reassuring and comforting. In fact, it was quite a relief. It was that you, as a regular American, don't have do anything radically different because you have not been doing anything wrong. You have simply been let down: your government has been incompetent and corrupt, elites are lining their pockets and leading you by the nose, even allies are taking advantage of you by not contributing to their national defense and through bad trade deals, and environmentalists are imposing job destroying restrictions on companies. Don't worry, you can go on digging coal and working in your factory just like before and I will protect you.

Step 4: Trial Closing

With all of the buying motivations defined and addressed it is good sales practice to attempt what is known as a trial closing. Something like, "will delivery in one week fit your schedule?" or "do you prefer the blue or the green?" This is a lot more comfortable than asking the customer to sign a piece of paper, but it can ease him into the mode of actually feeling that the sale is now more or less inevitable. Trump's trial closure took the form of rallies where he was able to throw out proposals and then gauge the crowd's reaction. A favorable response was a good sign that it would be something other followers would also support.

Although many did not see it at the time, the rallies underlined a very important fact—one also being confirmed by focus groups across the country: other presidential candidates who were trotting out their version of the party line or putting proposals on their websites were missing the point. This election would not be won with tired old ideas from insincere people or outlines of promises on websites. It would be won by the candidate who was able to successfully uncover, understand, and validate the insecurities of large sections of the population and then convince them that he was the only leader capable and strong enough to put things right. Trump hit the right emotional buttons and "sold the feeling" that "closed the deal".

After-Sales Service
Of course, making the sale only gets you part way there because the deal requires that the terms of the agreement have to be fulfilled. In politics this is the stage at which problems start because reality can become somewhat stubborn, and it often refuses to acquiesce to pre-election rhetoric.

An impartial observer could easily make the case that Donald Trump's fulfillment of promises has been something of a mixed bag. The following is a partial list of promises made:

Mexico Pay for Border Wall	No, and not funded by Congress.
Obamacare Repeal and Replace	No, better and cheaper health care nowhere in sight
Make sure $1 trillion infrastructure plan will be revenue neutral	No
Tax simplification in which largest reductions will be for the middle class	No - more complex and cuts largely for business and the wealthy
Deficit reduction	No - tax cuts and big increases in budget - headed for bigger deficits
Trade Deals	New name and minor changes to NAFTA
Leave Paris Climate Accord	Done
Conservative Supreme Court	Done
Bomb ISIS	Done
Ban Muslims	Partial
Move Israeli Embassy	Done
Remove Troops From Afghanistan	No
Deport All Illegal Immigrants	No

Leave NATO	No
Declare China to be a Currency Manipulator	No
Torture Terrorists	No
Create at least 10 million jobs in first term	Not on track—monthly average no better than Obama years
Grow the economy 4 percent per year	No. 2.3% for 2017
End defense sequester and expansion military investment	Done
Establish tariffs to discourage offshoring of jobs	Done
Cancel unconstitutional Obama executive actions	Partial
Protect vital infrastructure from cyber attack	No
End common Core	Partial
Impose complete ban on foreign lobbyists raining money for U.S. elections	No
Ethics reforms to reduce corrupting influence of special interests	No
Constitutional amendment to impose Congressional term limits	No
New screening procedures for immigration to ensure those admitted share our values	No
Reduce surging crime, drugs and violence	New policies but not enough data to prove they are working
Increase funding for programs that train and assist local police	Started
Reform visa rules to ensure jobs are offered to American workers first	Started
Establish two-year mandatory minimum federal prison sentence for illegally entering the U.S. after a previous deportation	Yes
Enhance visa rules to enhance penalties for overstaying	No enhanced penalties but increased activity

Establish a five-year mandatory minimum federal prison sentence for illegally re-entering for those with felony convictions, multiple misdemeanor convictions	No
Make 2 and 4 year college more affordable	No
Cancel all federal funding to sanctuary cities	No
Cancel visas to foreign countries that will not take back criminal illegal immigrants	Yes
Begin removing the more than 2 million criminal illegal immigrants	Started
Lift restrictions on fossil fuel industry	Yes
Provide matching contributions for low income families to the dependent care savings accounts	No
Require that for every federal regulation, two existing regulations must be eliminated	Yes
Allow American corporations to bring back profits at 10% rate	Yes
Create tax-free dependent care savings accounts for young and elderly dependents	No
Incentivize employers to provide on-site child-care services	No
Lower the business tax rate from 35% to 10%	No, actual cut was to 21%
Allow tax deductions for child and elder care	No
Reduce number of tax brackets from seven to three	No
Allow the purchase of health insurance across state lines	Yes
Give middle class families with two children a 35% tax cut	Yes, but there is a sunset provision
Provide veterans with the ability to receive attend private doctor of their choice	Started
Let states manage Medicaid funds	No
Replace Obamacare with savings accounts	No
Impose extreme vetting on all people coming into the country	Yes

Suspend immigration from terror-prone regions where vetting cannot occur	Partial
Cut red tape at FDA to speed up approval of new drugs	Yes
Stop billions in payments to U.N. Climate change programs and use the money to fix America's water and environmental infrastructure	Partial - money not going to U.N. but not being redirected to infrastructure
Increase resources to federal law enforcement to dismantle criminal gangs	Yes
Direct the secretary of commerce and U.S. trade representative to identify all foreign trading abuses that unfairly impact American workers	Yes, but no change
Direct the secretary of commerce and U.S. trade representative to use every tool under American and international law to end foreign trading abuses immediately	Yes
Expand vocational and technical education	Yes
Redirect education money to give parents the right to send their kid to the public, private, charter, magnet, religious or home school of their choice	Started
Create a task force on violent crime	Yes
Impose a lifetime ban on White House officials lobbying on behalf of a foreign government	Yes
Lift the Obama-Clinton roadblocks and allow vital energy infrastructure projects, like the Keystone Pipeline, to move forward	Yes
Withdraw from the Trans-Pacific-Partnership	Done
Impose a 5 year ban on White House and Congressional officials becoming lobbyists after leaving government service	No

Success, it would appear, is in the eye of the beholder. With all the activity and noise surrounding immigration and the economy, it is hard to identify numbers to support the contention that things are a hugely improved relative to the Obama years. Asylum seeking has increased, but Obama was a very active exporter of criminal aliens, and that has not changed too much. And the economy as demonstrated by job and GDP growth just looks like a straight-line projection of what was happening before the election. Healthcare has not been made better or more affordable, so not much change there, either. There have been a number of changes, though. The courts have many more right of center judges, environmental protections, including attempts to remediate climate change have either ended or been severely curtailed. And there have been huge tax cuts and the deficit is projected to increase dramatically.

Continued Support
No one expects perfection, but you would imagine that failure to deliver on key parts of Trump's platform like an economy expanding at 4%, deficit reduction, and improved health care would be sufficiently important to the base supporters that they would now be expressing some disappointment. Apparently not. It is clear that Trump's voter base has not lost faith, and they remain emotionally invested in the overall message. When Trump fails to deliver he is seen as doing his best and prevented by others from carrying through—typically either Democrats or Republicans in Congress. And of course the average supporter has never been alone—they have been encouraged to stay loyal by Fox News and right wing pundits working through the radio, internet and various social media outlets. Reinforcing the message that left wing media and the elites are still the enemy has successfully kept the team together.

It is fairly easy to get over some missed targets, but the administration seems to have some serious management issues. Even casual observance of daily news coverage provides us with a steady stream of problem areas, such as: sending out contradictory and incoherent messages; making statements that bear little resemblance to the truth; and having a leader with a reputation for having disdain for long-term planning, ignoring detailed facts, and actively discouraging bad news. There is an outside possibility that all of that is a rumor put about by political foes, but the continual churn in senior White House personnel supports the poor leadership reputation and cannot be easily dismissed because it is factual. Failure to maintain a coherent and competent senior management team in which members are given authority to execute their allotted tasks is <u>always</u> a sign that the head of the team is failing in his primary function. It appears that we elected a salesman, not a leader, and certainly not a manager.

It is clear that Donald Trump's consummate sales capability was the main reason he was successful in his quest to become president, but that does not explain everything. The next question concerns how he managed to retain support within the Republican Party for so long when many of his policy positions and behaviors have shown themselves to be antithetical to core Republican principles. The party traditionally upheld what was described as "values" which were understood to mean traditional Western morals that kept families together. The fact that this thrice-married philanderer abused women and paid others off to keep their extramarital relationships secret simply did not matter anymore. Lying about serious matters and even trivial issues did not matter either. Even playing fast and loose with national security turned out to be of little concern. For previous presidents cozying up to Russia and praising the leader of North Korea would have had congressmen apoplectic at any time in the recent past, but Trump got a pass from Republican members. The deficit was a major concern for both parties before the election and particularly so for the Republicans, but after the election the deficit was put on a trajectory to be vastly increased because of tax cuts and increased spending—all of a sudden deficits do not seem to matter anymore.

Clearly, something is going on that is difficult to explain. It could be that many grassroots Republicans have come to the conclusion that having the Presidency and both chambers of Congress is the only way to make sure the country stays on a conservative path, and tolerating Trump is just something we will have to put up with. After all, we have tax cuts, a right wing Supreme Court, and a pro-business administration. However, that is a cynical explanation that might work for serious political minds, but sounds a bit too analytical for the majority of people.

A more likely explanation is that Trump's list of grievances zeroed in on some real emotional issues that had resonance with people because they highlighted dangers to the very fabric of our nation.

Trump certainly did a good job convincing people that he understood their fears and that he was the person to lead the nation to a better and safer future. But that was just the first step. He then went on to create a bond with his followers by making it clear that outside forces were out to prevent him from helping them and stymie his mission to Make America Great Again. Those bent on defeating him included: elites of both parties, the FBI, the DOJ, left-wing courts, mainstream media, foreigners, and the "deep state", and even our own national security agencies. There was clearly a conspiracy underway, so critical opinions and facts produced by virtually any sort of organization could be dismissed as "fake." Such conspiracy theories might have been dismissed if made by Trump alone but this time it was different. Many right-wing pundits have taken up the Trump cause and lent legitimacy to the idea that the establishment in its various forms want to get rid of Trump. The conspiracy theory was, therefore, validated and made more mainstream.

One of our most important survival strategies as a species has been always been our innate desire to form groups to fend off danger and maintain group cohesion. We might not always entirely agree with the leader or even the rest of the group, but once we are emotionally involved we stay loyal, even when evidence and simple logic would suggest going against the group or just giving up. Difficulties do not automatically bring about the breakup of a committed group. In fact, being attacked only serves to make the group even tighter. As illustrated by the Kavanaugh hearings. This is why criticism and even fact-based arguments from the establishment in all its forms actually strengthened Trump supporters' resolve since it served to confirm that there was an attack underway and that there really was a conspiracy to shut the movement down.

Once the support was emotionally embedded it became not only strong, but durable because it was forged by some of our deepest human emotions, and on the political stage they win every time. The election and continuing support for Donald Trump should not, therefore, come as too much of a surprise.

The Good, the Bad, and the Ugly
To date, the results have been a mixture of successes and failures. Trump has done us the great service of identifying some deep concerns amongst much of the population and proven that the tired old messages from the established parties can and should be challenged. Not only that, he showed us that many other institutions need a wake-up call too. For example, in its search for ratings and revenue the media has slipped into the mode of exciting, entertaining, and feeding their customer base what they want to hear. Educational establishments have gotten more and more left-wing to the point that any opinion that does not conform with their progressive agenda is derided as almost Neanderthal and unworthy of discussion. Identifying concerns and overturning the elite's apple cart is good, but it is only the start. It is important to understand people's worries and concerns, but the focus should be on identifying the real underlying problems, formulating plans to resolve them, and then ensuring that the execution results in success.

Although Donald Trump has done a good job of identifying many concerns in the country, he has failed to identify the nation's key challenges. After the election his main focus has been pleasing supporters with actions that appear to have momentum, but lack the rigor of well-disciplined management. Trump's signature way of identifying emotionally driven fears and then adopting a "wing-it" management style has taken confusion and ineptitude to a whole new level.

Trump has generated more acrimony, confusion, and outright panic than any president in recent memory, and this could lead us into making some ill-advised choices in the future. There are those who have bought into the Trump message who will likely continue to support him, but there are likely many more who have been horrified by the spectacle and want to get back to normal. This is an unsatisfactory course of action since future candidates will return to being chosen on the basis of outdated and ideologically driven priorities rather than the real needs of the country and the government will continue to be poorly managed. Clearly not a path to competence and real wealth creation.

Can we take the best of Trump and then come up with something better?

Chapter 3

Dysfunctional Politics

Our Biggest Problem: We Are Human

Why do we notice and then follow shiny objects, get bored, and then start looking for the next glimmer in the distance? The simple answer is that we are humans and we are always on the lookout for something different that looks good and holds the promise of solving all of our problems. In the retail world this process is wasteful, but it keeps our economy moving—new cell phone, anyone? Unfortunately, our political system allows and even encourages us to do the same thing, with some positive results but some that have profoundly negative impacts. Rightly or wrongly, we have constructed a democratic political system that gives citizens the power to form groups of like-minded people and elect anyone who claims to have the magic bullet, in a process that embodies humanity's strengths and weaknesses. The biggest group of voters controls the destiny of society—typically getting what they want, if not necessarily what they really <u>need</u>.

"Government of the people, by the people, for the people" sounds like a good and simple maxim for a properly functioning society. Unfortunately, getting it to work is not that easy, and making it work efficiently is incredibly difficult. You would think it would be a simple matter of finding out what people want and then making it happen. The trouble is that humans are difficult and complex creatures. For a start, consensus is rare, so the will of the majority must be forced onto the minority. We also change our minds, do not always know what is really going on, or even understand the question being asked. We get locked into our group's way of thinking, get excited about the wrong things, and find it difficult to control our emotions. If we are to make a serious attempt at improving our democracy, we should recognize who we are and then design a system that accommodates our humanity. We have brains superior to those of any other animal on the planet and our main claim to fame is that we can think logically, but that does not mean we make all of our decisions based on logic—far from it.

If we are to adjust our political system to accommodate how we think and behave it is important to understand our background as a species. Evolution has made us who we are today: a highly adaptable species that has remained much the same as it was somewhere between 70,000 and 100,000 years ago when our ancestors moved out of Africa.

When you think about it, maybe we really don't do that badly. After all, it seems unlikely that a species with the attributes necessary to succeed as hunter-gatherers would be ideally suited to our modern data-rich digital age. Evolution only really got us to the point that we could organize ourselves into groups and hunt for food. So maybe it is not surprising that many aspects of modern life do not correlate with some of our basic human instincts. For example, since food was scarce during much of human history, evolution drove us to create an environment that provided us with reliable food sources with as little physical labor as possible. Unfortunately, we have found that our drive to eat as much high-calorie food as we can certainly works against us now that it is available at all times. Furthermore, sitting at a desk all day, driving everywhere, and watching TV in the evening is a life of leisure and luxury unimaginable years ago—but we now know that it is killing us. It is clear that our minds and bodies do not match today's environment. It is as though we haven't caught up with the reality of our modern way of life. The fact is we all now have the freedom to choose a healthy lifestyle, but it is a constant battle with our built-in instincts that were developed to survive as hunters-gatherers.

Our instinctual compulsion to overeat and avoid exercise are just a couple of examples of how our inherited brains sometimes push us to behave in ways that are not in our long-term best interests. Our instincts manifest themselves in our conscious brains as instantaneous reactions like "fight or flight" in a dangerous situation and as an emotional reaction or "feeling" resulting from what we see, hear, feel, or even smell. As a species, we collected these instinctual responses because they ensured our survival.

Through the rigors of evolution, humans developed huge brains and an unparalleled ability to adapt and thrive in practically any environment. That tremendous increase in mental ability was necessary for our human ancestors to cooperate and progressively learn from each successive generation, so that communities could become increasingly successful and likely to survive. Communication skills became an important survival mechanism that our ancestors were able to use to collaborate on new ideas to mitigate present and future potential dangers.

But then, of course, it became much more complicated. Within a group there had to be ways of ensuring that lessons learned were actually put into practice. Simple behaviors like how to find a game trail and successfully ambush animals would have been easy to adopt because the benefits could easily be seen and the rewards were immediately obvious—food meant survival. But what about the more complicated stuff, such as when and where to move camp, who mates with whom, who owns what, and how do we prepare for winter? And what about the things that are really difficult to explain, like when will the rains come, why does game disappear and the sun come over the horizon? Having a larger brain was clearly a double-edged sword. A brain capable of reasoning and making plans to handle the vagaries of weather and behaviors of other humans would not simply accept authority without an intelligible reason to do so. With so much happening there had to be more than a simple wolf-like social structure.

Our early human ancestors likely had a social structure based on physical strength since they could use that power to dominate weaker members of the group. To a certain extent, that made a lot of sense because a strong body was a good demonstration of genes worth passing on. As with all things human it was likely not that simple for long. The ability to think things through, explain issues and proposed actions likely attracted a following that could be more powerful than one single strong and aggressive person. The ability of humans to build alliances and assemble groups of like-minded people was a natural successor. The immediate family groups could then expand to include other people who had similar beliefs and ways of living. In that way, people living many miles away could be identified with because they were members of the same tribe.

There are many examples of solitary animals surviving successfully throughout the world. But being part of a pack or herd has many advantages over a solitary existence, and the numbers of creatures adopting this organizational structure prove that this is also a winning survival strategy. Some cooperative creatures like bees and ants have developed highly complex systems for working together to a common end, but each individual really only responds to chemical and physical stimuli. There is no individual thinking going on per se, but it works.

Herd animals are a step up from insects. Elephants are unusually intelligent herd animals that have developed complex social structures and ways of communicating. But for many herd species the main reason for keeping together is to have extra pairs of eyes to spot potential dangers. Clearly, the solitary, pack, and herd animals in all their various forms that exist today have all passed the evolutionary test—they have survived. And so did we, but in a more complex way. We were able to develop a consensus and act with a common purpose.

Although there are countless ways of clinging to life in this world, there is one strategy that stands out as being the most successful of all in terms of the ability of a species to control its own destiny: humans cooperating with each other, with all of the difficulties and complications that involves. It should not come as a big surprise, therefore, that nature preprogrammed human brains to handle all of the vagaries of living with each other and taking on the outside world. But it does not end there. Just like the behaviors of dogs described in Chapter 1, we are not simply the prisoners of the genes we were born with—that is just the start. We are also deeply affected by our early education/ experiences and then by the circumstances in which we find ourselves.

Genetics

Our prehuman ancestors in Africa adapted from living in trees to walking biped-ally and then contended with a continually changing environment that oscillated between wet and dry, and hot and cold for millions of years. It is this rapidly changing climatic environment that was likely the big push towards developing the bigger brains that became the essential tool in the struggle to adapt. Evolution winnowed out various human-like contenders who were not able to compete in the race to prove who could produce the most effective communal strategy to contend with continual environmental changes that were being thrust upon them. The ones left (literally) standing were modern humans. By this time, our brains had developed the necessary attributes for a successful communal existence. Human babies did not have to learn all that was necessary for tribal living—millions of years of evolution had hardwired those fundamentals into the brain before birth.

Clearly, life was not only about picking fruit, sitting around, and hugging each other. Although there was a built-in desire to cooperate, by today's standards life was still indescribably tough. Food would be in short supply at times, there would be constant jostling for power, the climate would change, and there would likely be other groups of humans to compete with. The human brain required multiple innate capabilities and responses built in so that the appropriate actions could be adopted when a particular situation occurred.

The range of innate human feelings and predispositions is vast, and in many instances they separate us from most other creatures. In no particular order they include:

Self-awareness
Group affiliation
Respect for social order
Loyalty
Religion
Desire to build
Desire to destroy
Willingness to kill
Willingness to steal
Desire for peace
Morality
Empathy
Cruelty
Anger
Love
Hate
Fear
Loathing
Selfishness
Altruism
Disgust
Suspicion
Trust
Fairness
Desperation
Skepticism
Habit formation
Lust
Embarrassment
Honesty
Deviousness
Pattern recognition
Quest to understand

Persistence
Lassitude
Curiosity
Spirituality
Fear of the unfamiliar
Etc, Etc.

The capacity for these emotions and propensity for certain behaviors has been built into our brains for the simple reason that at times in our evolutionary history they were necessary for us to survive. They almost all have a place in our survival repertoire so that they can come forth when necessary. The problem is that it is not always clear when and how they should be called upon. For the most part it is society that makes the rules. For example, apart from when necessary for the maintenance of law and order, our tendency to be violent and kill other humans is restricted to performing military duties. In which case those who carry out violent acts are lauded as exemplary citizens.

Education and Experiences

Humans live in a complicated social world and understanding how it works can be extremely painful—just ask middle school kids and their parents. Having to navigate the nuances of what words and actions really mean requires some impressive brainpower. Anyone who has sent an email that has been misinterpreted understands that words alone do not always convey the intended message. Face-to-face communication is always better, but even then things can go awry. Social pressures push us into becoming adept at controlling and hiding or even misrepresenting our feelings, and this makes for a complex interpersonal world.

Our education starts from the moment we are born—maybe even earlier when we were in the womb, picking up on subtle vibrations. Indeed, some believe that early formation of language capabilities begins in utero. Babies start to be social animals very early on and there is a theory that after a few weeks they even start to "lie" to elicit the desired response from their mother.

Bending the truth in its strictest sense becomes very much a part of life as we learn to navigate the complex world of human relationships. If we are always completely honest life gets difficult very quickly, so we learn to avoid those pitfalls with various disguises, such as facial expressions, body movements, vocal tones, and words. What we are trying to do is get what we want without disturbing the group too much. And we shouldn't feel ashamed—it is so much a part of our humanity that it must be an essential part of human survival. Our informal education has, in large part, got a great deal to do with interaction with other people. We constantly feel the consequences of others' actions through personal interactions and the imposition of society's application of rules. The other important part of our informal education comes from learning about the outside world including basic physics like: gravity, speed, heat, and sharpness are learned through activities like playing games, carrying and dropping heavy things, and burning fingers with matches, etc. As children we often experience both unfortunate and pleasurable events in the company of others so these group experiences add to the agreed knowledge base that will be necessary for ensuing stages of life.

Our formal educational system tends to be more structured and less exciting than life outside of academia, but it is just a variation of the age-old process of passing the collective wisdom of the tribe onto the next generation. Some of it requires a lot of hard work and mental concentration, but it is necessary if we are to prepare ourselves for the next big challenge that the world throws our way. Formal education is the passing on of essential truths from one person or generation onto the next, but what might appear to be right and true to one person was not always accepted as true by another. Indeed, many accepted absolute truths have later been found to have no foundation in reality at all. In a sense, that really did not always matter to early civilizations in the short-term since it was more important for them to fashion their own beliefs in order to achieve a common vision and societal cohesion when facing new challenges. But there had to be a mechanism in place to question accepted dogma and then make appropriate changes. After all, ignoring the truth for too long would eventually result in failure or being taken over by a competing tribe that had better ideas.

Circumstances

Having all of the innate responses listed above built into our brains and then having them molded to suit our own personal environment and experiences seems like a pretty good formula for success as a tribal-based culture. But people's thoughts and actions cannot be understood without properly considering the effect of circumstances.

Circumstances can change everything. It is true that a man might investigate a dumpster for food when he is hungry or be prepared to shoot someone if threatened, but these are reflexive responses to immediate personal discomfort or danger. What is more difficult to see is the change of mindset that occurs when circumstances change on a societal scale.

When people feel comfortably in control of their lives they tend to be open to other people and ideas and disposed to generosity of spirit. If things change and there is an environment of danger from physical attack, hunger, loss of a job, reduction in status, etc. people tend to have a completely different outlook on life. A loss of security explains why people and eventually entire societies appear to change their character.

The 20th century German experience gives us a graphic example of how deeply a nation can be affected by experience and circumstance. How could the most educated and civilized country in Europe become the brutish thug that swept through Europe and Russia with so little regard for human life that they would kill and even try to exterminate those considered to be of inferior races? Before Hitler's rise to power, the German Jewish population was one of the most integrated in Europe, with most

Jews considering themselves as Germans first and Jews second. And Germany had one of the highest rates of Jew/Gentile intermarriage in Europe. They then seemed to go from civilized to heartless racists bent on world domination. In the post-war era the Germans went on to become the people we know today: socially liberal pacifists who are supremely successful exporters and defenders of fiscal rectitude. How did it all happen?

After the First World War many Germans felt betrayed by their politicians and Jews because they felt they had been betrayed while good patriotic soldiers were sacrificing all for the Fatherland. The country also suffered terribly from an economy characterized by rampant inflation brought on in part by the Allies' demands for reparations. In an environment of resentment, economic collapse, and a feeling of betrayal Hitler was able to craft a message of anti liberal democracy, racial intolerance and world domination that would not have resonated at all had the circumstance been different. The post Second World War period was very different. Firstly, the citizens knew they were beaten and there was no one else to blame, and the Allies did not demand financial reparations. In fact, America stepped in and provided cash via the Marshall Plan, which helped the West German economy to blossom. It was this new and secure environment that transformed the Germans back into being the model citizens of Europe. There are lessons to be learned. The 20th Century has provided us with a graphic illustration of how humans can readily revert to their lowest barbaric instincts when societies fail to provide the basic levels of security necessary for civilized life. It is not human nature that keeps us prosperous and protects us from savagery—it is the careful nurturing of our societies.

What is true for nations and communities is true for all individuals. When people exhibit what appears to be moral weakness, or do things that are detrimental to themselves and others the cause can generally be traced back to insecurity in one form or another. Insecure people do not make good decisions.

Rational Thought

Genetics, education, experience, and circumstances together control much of our daily lives. But every now and then rational thought enters the picture in an attempt to assimilate new things and sort out what seems to be a bit odd. We also try to establish patterns in what we see and make plans for the future.

How and when is it appropriate to stop and think? Sitting down and solving a mathematical equation clearly requires logical thought. But sometimes we have to address issues of a moral nature. Unless we have relevant data there are no mathematical equations to answer such questions. Since the birth of civilization humans have struggled with the interplay of emotions and logic —or as it used to be known: *passion* and *reason.*

Plato believed that passions should be kept under control and that a man should always strive to ensure that reason becomes the master of passions. He felt so strongly about this that he believed that if a man failed to do so he would be reincarnated as a woman. Benjamin Franklin had a somewhat more nuanced view, believing that passions and reason had their places but they often fought against each other and should be handled carefully. David Hume, an 18th century Scottish philosopher, appears to have postulated a theory that is close to what the most recent scientific studies tell us: in any thought battle in our brains, emotion will almost always overcome rational thought. That sounds scary and almost incomprehensible, but it appears to have been essential to our survival as a species.

Passions, Emotions, and Ethics

At this point, a clarification of the terms "passions", "emotions", "innate ethics" and "intuitive ethics" is in order. For the purpose of this book they are terms used interchangeably and intended to describe the combination of inherited characteristics and learned beliefs and ethics that form the basis of a person's concept of what constitutes the truth, how we should behave, and what is right and wrong for the community.

Once our ethics have been embedded into our subconscious we can then react quickly and precisely to any event or situation in which we find ourselves. From an evolutionary perspective this makes sense. Once we have a society with rules that work for us we do not want to start a brand new philosophical argument every time something slightly different happens. That would be wasteful in terms of time and energy and likely result in inconsistency and confusion potentially leading to anarchy and failure.

Thought Auto-Pilot

If an issue arises that challenges our conditioned beliefs, our brain approaches the problem on a somewhat hierarchical basis, each one influencing the next. Once new circumstances have been absorbed by the subconscious, the brain looks for an appropriate response from its bank of intuitive ethics—those deeply held moral principles that began as genetic predispositions and were subsequently molded by personal experience and societal norms. The next step is to see how, or even if, they can be applied. If the circumstances are significantly disruptive behavior-driving ethics can be temporarily affected, and sometimes changed for generations. People who find themselves without sufficient money to feed their family might consider stealing food, but regain their moral rectitude when things get back to normal. But the German situation leading up to the Second World War was more long term. It caused a profound and pervasive change in its citizen's attitudes towards racism and brutality, and because it lasted for an extended period of time it became part of the culture. The post-war environment was different again, and it fostered a more civilized culture.

As a last resort, we might take a look at an issue using our powers of rational thought. In a serious flight-or-fight situation there really isn't much choice. When we actually do have an opportunity to think about a moral question we often still gravitate to our innate beliefs—and when called upon to explain why, we typically search for arguments to support the contention we have already formulated. It then looks and feels as though we have thought about the issue, but all we have really done is reaffirm our originally held moral stance.

Evolution has, in effect, left us with a pretty good mechanism for establishing and then policing moral and behavioral standards and then making sure we all keep to the rules—or bend them if survival is threatened. This process is particularly effective in small isolated groups because every person can be scrutinized for compliance. Furthermore, new ideas do not crop up very often so the community is able to maintain its homogeneity of thought. Larger societies find it much more difficult to maintain homogeneity of thought because groups of like-minded people tend to live separate lives but occasionally the groups interact with each other. Such interaction can result in conflict, but over time it can also lead to a society that is more accepting of new ideas and tolerant of people with different ideas and ways of life. Mixing with others who have different views and lifestyles very often leads to the conclusion that there really is no danger, and new ideas can be beneficial.

Change and Progress

Societal change and progress come from either: habituation—simply getting used to something that makes things better or worse; or by analyzing issues and making rational decisions as to what changes should be made. Sometimes changes happen as a mixture of both.

Homosexuality was once feared and loathed in much of Western society, and there were laws in place to support the public's view that it was detrimental to society. But with the passage of time straight and gay people got to know each other personally, and found that they often became good friends. Once they discovered that homosexuals were not a danger to society it became possible to accept homosexuality as just one more aspect of human life. Whether they believed it was brought about genetically or as a lifestyle choice, it really didn't matter. With public support, the government then stepped in and made laws that applied a principle of common law which states that you can do whatever you like so long as you are not harming others. The next step went beyond just repealing laws making homosexual acts illegal—it fashioned laws that actually prevent discrimination on the basis of being LBGT. Who would have thought that possible 20 or 30 years ago?

Another example is that of smoking bans in practically all public places, which came slowly at first and would not have become universal without the support of some segments of the population and government action. The government in many locations took the position that if you have a rule that says you can't ask people to work in unsafe areas (and second-hand smoke is injurious to your health) smoking in almost all public places had to stop. Whether you agree with the ban or not, there is logic to the argument—so it became one of those examples of society reviewing the data and making subsequent new rules. The rules are well accepted and now it is hard to imagine any other way.

But change is not always welcome, and wanting to keep things the same is perfectly natural. After all, if something is working, why would you change? Indeed, some of the ingrained attitudes we were born with were put there by evolution so that we would not opt for change without a demonstrably good reason. Even small changes could result in disaster. But surely we could exercise the logical part of our brains to analyze our current situation, predict the future, and then figure out that old answers are not necessarily going to work? Yes, we could, but it is much more comfortable hearing that we don't have to change our opinion too much.

The process of evolution fashioned us into who we are today and made all of our advancements possible. There were many false steps along the way and many species of early hominids disappeared because they did not possess the necessary mental attributes to form viable and enduring societies. Evolution is a hard taskmaster that has no particular preference for any variation—but it does demand success. Along with our reasoning capabilities, it appears that having inheritable moral ethics was a winning strategy. How do we know that for certain? Quite simply, if it were not so, we would not be the people we are today.

Modern Humans

So here we are—a species with a built-in set of ethics, the ability to learn, and the mental capacity to solve problems.

Since the early days when Homo sapiens moved out of Africa things haven't changed too much when it comes to utilitarian items. Figuring out how to make tools for everyday tasks has been something humans have been very good at right from the start. And modern technologies have provided us with all the wonders and life-enhancing products we experience every day of our lives. It isn't that we have become more intelligent over the years, it is that we have been able to recognize what works, and then build on that knowledge from one generation to the next. It is a process that readily draws on our intellectual capabilities because when something demonstrably works and is useful, the next step is to see if it can improved. In that sense, a new type of microchip is no different from attaching a piece of sharp flint to the tip of an arrow.

But there are other kinds of analyses that have never been quite so easy. What works spiritually and socially is still a challenging issue because the cause and effects are very difficult to see right away. If there is a disagreement regarding something that is—by its very nature—unprovable, why do we instinctually grab onto an idea and cling to it and make it our "truth"? One reason could be that humans have always attempted to see patterns in everything they experience. Even in the absence of scientific data we have to have some sort of explanation for what is happening in the world around us. And there was no shortage of inexplicable phenomena in pre-human days. A search for the causes of physical happenings such as: the rising of the sun, thunder, and abundance of game, could generate multiple explanations. Maybe it was the way the sacrifice was made, and perhaps the gods are angry because an established rule was broken, etc., etc. It likely didn't matter which one you picked, but so long as a majority went for the same one, the tribe would be peaceful and quiet. Developing consensus even on issues that were unprovable thereby created a disciplined and consistent response to uncontrollable circumstances. And like all aspects of human development, it has stayed with us because it worked. It is somewhat different now, however, because we live in much bigger and diverse societies so our "tribe" is just a part of the whole—comprised of the people around us—usually the ones we work and socialize with.

In his book *"The Righteous Mind: Why Good People Are Divided by Politics and Religion"* Johnathon Haidt gives a detailed, but readable, account of why people hold differing views and what effects it has on societies. It might be surprising to learn that we tend to attach ourselves to political causes and ideas for reasons that go beyond self-interest.

In America, we tend to divide ourselves into conservative and liberal camps. Conservatives tend to be motivated by:

- Loyalty - to groups, e.g., family, nation
- Authority - Respect for order and discipline, e.g. police, military
- Sanctity - desire to lead a better life, e.g. religion, fear of contamination
- Liberty - freedom from imposed power, e.g. government, other nations

But liberals concentrate on:

- Care - empathy for others e.g., poor and oppressed
- Fairness - to ensure there is justice e.g., protection of human rights, equal pay/equal work

Note that conservatives tend to have a slightly different view of fairness. They are not so much concerned with outcomes, but like to see equal opportunity and proportional rewards that reflect effort and success.

Oddly enough, we support ideas and moral positions because we feel it is good for the group with which we identify ourselves. We reflexively align ourselves with people like us, even if that might be detrimental to our personal situation. For example, there are many wealthy liberals who would be happy to pay more taxes if that would result in a better life for poor people and society in general. On the other hand, there are many poor whites who disdain social programs that would benefit them and make them healthier and more financially secure.

Clearly there are many overlaps, but the more liberal or conservative you are, the more accurate the above list will be for predicting what will be hot-button issues for you and what type of presentation will appeal to you the most.

Haidt explains that taking up and sticking to sides makes sense from an evolutionary perspective since it promotes solidarity and consistency. But he also describes the downside, which is that a civil discourse can become difficult and sometimes nearly impossible. Oftentimes, we shut down our critical thinking capabilities and take a position because we think it is what our group would approve of or expect. Haidt makes the analogy of our logical brain contorting itself into believing the "party line" so that it can then act as the press secretary to rationalize and then spread the message.

All of which goes straight to some long standing fundamental political disagreements. For example, have you ever wondered why the subject of climate change elicits completely different responses from the right and left? How could such an important issue that involves our quality of life and science degenerate into a partisan issue? You would think that a person's opinion on the topic would be separate from their overall political views, but it isn't. It could be that climate change challenges some of our fundamental beliefs. Perhaps those on the left see it as just another issue requiring cooperative action that cannot be handled by individuals so it must be handed over to the government—and our collective welfare requires that strenuous action must be taken even if large expenditures and a major dislocation of the economy is required. Perhaps it is different for those on the right because they start with a mindset that the government should only get involved in anything as a last resort and the free market should not be manipulated. A well-functioning economy is fundamental to our well-being and the government cannot be trusted to make decisions for individuals. Furthermore, as well as impacting the overall economy, large-scale government actions will by their very nature affect personal freedoms. It appears that despite all the information available we do not rely on facts alone.

As Simon and Garfunkel tell us in "The Boxer": *"All lies and jests, still a man hears what he wants to hear, And disregards the rest"*

It would seem that our intuitive ethics have now assumed even more power than they used to. It could be that we are so overwhelmed by data that to make things comprehendible we revert to relying on what we "know." But that really isn't getting us very far because we spend more time disagreeing and supporting our arguments with the facts we choose to believe, rather than thinking rationally. We then formulate all sorts of rationales for our positions that are fashioned to appeal to people like us, without much regard for the opinions and motivations of those on the other side of the fence. All of this detracts from what we should really be doing, which is agreeing on common goals and then formulating plans to achieve those goals. Unfortunately, that requires the hard work to identify what are pleasant, but empty, blue-sky promises, and also being honest enough to question some basic beliefs.

It is, therefore, not surprising that our political system leaves us open to manipulation—for the simple reason that we keep acting like humans. We are a soft touch for politicians who appeal to our emotions in one way or another, because when it comes to social issues we readily go for what sounds comfortable and easy, particularly when the appeal is made to people like us.

As well as simply giving our votes to candidates who promise a sure-fire way of giving us something for nothing, or protecting us from everything the world is likely to throw at us, we are particularly drawn to those who appeal to our preconceived notions of what is true. Once we join the team that appears to share our beliefs we do another human thing, we stick with our team. Which is all well and good so long as we are supporting an ideology that is actually providing the country with demonstrable benefits as opposed to what we simply want to hear. But to do something different requires looking beyond ego-soothing rhetoric and being more skeptical—and we generally don't like doing that.

Chapter 4

Rational Thought: Our Underused Asset

"Thinking is the hardest work there is, which is probably the reason why so few engage in it."

— Henry Ford

We humans are spectacularly different from other animals. No other creature has our mental capacity. It is our intellectual capabilities that have enabled us to create huge cooperative societies and alter our environment so successfully that we have been able to colonize the world. We have developed technologies that have relieved many of us from the dangers, drudgeries, and uncertainties imposed by the natural world that had always been an everyday part of life.

But, the application of logic is not simple even in areas of study that are subject to intense scientific rigor. You would think that when knowledge is built on scientific principles that have been corroborated by others, it would be possible to provide rock-solid answers to previously unanswered questions and also make accurate predictions for the future. After all, this process has been the foundation for all of the technological and scientific advances made in at least the last 300 years and has provided us with a quality of life that would have previously been unimaginable. Even in areas of study like astronomy, mathematics, physics, chemistry, and economics, which all inherently require a great deal of disciplined and logical thought, there have been opposing theories over the years. But established theories are not based on pure science alone. Different theories have often been supported by groups on opposite sides with a fervor that often went beyond what should be expected from a supposed competition between theories based on pure logic. History shows us that the opposing scientists would take up sides and often actively search for evidence to support their theories rather than search for the absolute truth. It appears as though <u>their</u> truth being proven right was more important than objective truth. This all seems strange because you would think that the trained scientific mind would ensure that logic would always prevail over emotions and partisan beliefs. Apparently not. For example, Australian doctor Barry Marshall had a theory that stomach ulcers were caused by bacteria, but it was an idea that was not well received by the medical establishment. As far as those in the know were concerned the matter had been settled many years ago. Stress was the cause and bland food was the answer. Dr. Marshall was either ignored or in some cases ridiculed because he challenged conventional science. Only after he took the matter into his own hands by drinking an infected concoction and then developing an ulcer did those in power take notice and eventually endorse his findings. Although this is an example of scientific people protecting their established beliefs the happy ending illustrates the real value of the scientific approach. People can hold onto whatever theory they like until it is proven to be incorrect by verifiable data—in other words the truth always wins in the end.

If emotions can get tangled up with the logic of science, it should come as no surprise that opinions regarding the politics of everyday life should become an almost impossible mix of reason and group-think advocacy. It is a complex interplay of almost unprovable cause-and-effect and the desire to enhance and protect our own group physically and morally.

We humans, therefore, have something of a split personality when it comes to thinking rationally. Although not perfect, we tend to be logical when solving business, physical, and technological problems, but only use our brain to confirm preconceptions when it comes to social issues. For many social issues this really doesn't matter at all. In the Western world the religion you practice is entirely personal and for the most part it does not affect others outside of your family. But other issues involve politics, which dictate social policy and that can have profound effects on other peoples' lives. Because we live in a democracy there is a constant ebb and flow with like-minded groups imposing their prejudices on the rest of society—some being happy, while others are not.

This tendency for a person to reflexively protect their own established "truths" likely worked well in homogeneous hunter-gatherer and agrarian societies, but it made progressively less sense as the industrial revolution took hold and the nature of burgeoning economies brought about huge changes.

We are now part of a global economy and well into the digital age. We find ourselves in a similar situation to the one our forebears experienced as industrialization gathered speed and destroyed jobs but created others. During the industrial revolution people were forced to find new types of work and adapt to very different lifestyles, so social policy had to change too. The changes all seemed very rapid at the time, but in reality the changes were somewhat sedate compared to what is happening today.

In today's world, every country has to compete. It is true that China does not play to rules in many ways, and that is unacceptable, but we should not allow that fact to deflect us from our primary mission which is to make ourselves more competitive. If we fail to accept reality and refuse to use our ability to analyze and discuss matters rationally we will be left behind as others prosper.

It will be a tall order in our currently poisoned political atmosphere, but the prescription is simple and clear. All we need to do is put our preconceptions to the side and utilize our most valuable yet underused asset—the ability to make rational choices and then mobilize the limitless resources of this great country.

Chapter 5

Where Are We?

"It was the best of times, it was the worst of times, it was the age of wisdom, it was the age of foolishness, it was the epoch of belief, it was the epoch of incredulity, it was the season of Light, it was the season of Darkness, it was the spring of hope, it was the winter of despair…"

— Charles Dickens, A Tale of Two Cities

The previous chapters are concerned with the battle between our innate emotions and logical thought, which is not a new phenomenon by any means. We are still trying to come to terms with how to push our politics away from the emotional side and towards a more logical approach to decision-making, but it is far from easy. Donald Trump more than any other president in recent history has shown us that a run for the presidency can still be hugely influenced by identifying and playing to deep-seated emotions.

It is hard to imagine that anyone would argue that Donald Trump has had a tremendous impact on our nation. Some are convinced that he is the worst thing that has ever happened to the country, while others believe that God had a hand in him becoming president. There certainly are some strong feelings, and experience tells us that the environment those feelings create almost always gets in the way of a logical analysis of what is really going on and formulating a plan for the future.

Let's be clear, Donald Trump did not invent divisiveness in society, but he does use it as part of an overall strategy to paint a picture of "people like us" being under attack. Such a proposition has been used to great effect in many countries for countless years, particularly if there is a feeling of dissatisfaction and insecurity. Although a good way to get people excited, it is not a good way to understand and then remedy the real underlying issues that are causing the insecurity. But let us not get too concerned about Donald Trump. He is neither the cause nor the solution to our current problems. They have been creeping up on us for quite some time—long before Trump even thought about getting into politics.

The Big Picture

The seeds of the present situation were being sown in the 1970s, but were not fully appreciated at the time. The impact of international competition was starting to be felt and it was becoming increasingly difficult for our domestic industries to compete—even the big ones like automobile manufacturing. Now we are in the digital age and everything has gathered momentum such that the world is now changing more rapidly than in any other time in history, and many aspects of life will never be the same. And it is serious. If we fail to recognize this new reality, we will all be left behind culturally and economically. History is littered with examples of societies that hung onto the old ways and ultimately withered away, and contrary to what some believe we have not been blessed with the divine right to remain the most prosperous nation on earth. Like any other country, we must adapt and compete or start a steady decline.

The economic turmoil that surfaced in 2008 highlighted some major problems, but it was more a symptom than the actual underlying problem. The causes of the recession were rooted in changes in technology and global trade together with unsustainable spending built on debt, both governmental and personal. The reason it snuck up on us was that the initial effects were not that unpleasant. You could go to Home Depot and pick up a tool that was half the price of what it used to be. That drop in prices for manufactured products was evident virtually everywhere. A customer could buy two of anything, go buy something else, or just save money. Most people chose the "buy something else" route—including houses. And this was facilitated by banks that gave easy credit at low interest rates. It got even better. The houses we bought were increasing in value because they were so easy to buy, so we could go and borrow even more money. This was clearly a very happy paradigm—for a while. The other shoe had to drop sooner or later, and it did. It happened when the house of cards that was built on people steadily increasing their debt without the ability to pay even the interest, let alone the principal, came crashing down. To make it worse, it became evident that the government had been racking up unsustainable debts as well.

The start of the 21st century has given us what some economists have called "a period of adjustment" in which the free market forces people, companies, and institutions to modify their expectations and behaviors to accommodate a new reality. That might be technically true, but it does not adequately describe the pain that people are suffering. It is particularly hard on people who have been playing by the rules: working hard, paying bills, and educating their kids. Even the good guys were not spared the devastating effects of the recession and its aftermath.

Unfortunately, many of our politicians have not risen to the challenge. Some have proposed finding out who needs help and then subsidizing the pain away. Others appear to think that the 2008 financial collapse was a normal recession, so if we lower taxes and cut entitlements, everything will be fine. Maybe, but it all seems so twentieth century. Trump proposed a twenty-first century solution that involved a bit of both previous century solutions: cutting taxes, increasing government spending, leaving entitlements alone, and blaming foreigners and domestic elites for all of our problems. And, by the way, you don't have to do anything differently, because I will look after you. It would appear that our new ideas are no better than the old ones.

Although it sometimes feels as though the whole world has been turned upside down, it is important to understand that the big things have not changed. Businesses still have to do what they have always done: identify customers, meet their needs, and make a profit. Employees must acquire the skills appropriate for the positions available and work hard and effectively for their companies. The government must collect tax revenue sufficient to pay for the services it provides. But the new reality is changing what the players can expect from each other.

One thing is for sure, we can't keep continuing on the same path. Our fundamental problems cannot get wished away by simply lowering taxes, subsidizing whoever or whatever is struggling, or simply blaming everyone else.

Our society is definitely beset with many problems, and we will just have to live with many of them. After all, we are humans and life will never be perfect. That does not mean that we should not attempt to identify the big seemingly intractable problems that, if not addressed urgently, will force us into a downward spiral. The following pages include justsome of the problems facing American society.

1. Wage Stagnation

There has been much written about why wages do not rise faster when unemployment numbers are relatively low. The simple answer appears to be that when the relative value of labor has gone down, and although there have been ups and downs, there is not enough consistent demand for employees to drive wages higher. Why is that? The most frequently proffered answer is that the high-wage manufacturing jobs that used to lift all labor wages have been transferred to low-wage countries. This theory can easily be supported by looking at the historical numbers. Since the end of the 1970s when we first started getting serious foreign competition in manufacturing, middle-wage workers have seen their paychecks increase by only 6% which is an annual increase of just 0.2%. But more recently, apart from the odd blip, the situation has gotten even worse for the middle class.

Although we have all benefited from lower prices, global competition has not helped increase wages in Western nations. What was once known as the Third World is now populated by developing countries that have become smarter and more productive. The West is no longer an island of technology, expertise, and wealth. Many Asian countries in particular have the advantage of productive, low-cost labor and they have made many industries like electronics and textiles into ones high-wage countries cannot compete with. Even China is finding it hard to compete with the likes of Vietnam because their own labor rates are rising. It is not a static situation either. Developing countries are also getting more adept at producing more sophisticated products.

The result has been that much of the work previously done in America can now be performed overseas. This has led to a reduction in demand for goods produced domestically, so lower pay and unemployment have been the inevitable results. Pay rates in these manufacturing industries used to be relatively high and they supported lower, but decent wages in the service sectors. High wages for unskilled and semiskilled work now appear to be a thing of the past. Whether people think it's all fair or not doesn't change reality. We have to figure out how to get ahead of the game by being globally competitive.

The increased use of technology to replace human labor just makes things worse. The digitized world has been brutal to many workers in well-established industries. This is, of course, the history of the industrialized world. Every new innovation has been good news for some and a disaster for others. Steam-powered looms destroyed home-based textile production in England in the early days of the Industrial Revolution, and horse-powered transportation industries took a big hit when gasoline engines arrived on the scene. There have been innumerable other examples throughout history.

New technologies would not be entertained if there were no advantages. In the business world, this often means a reduction in labor costs resulting in less demand for labor. This is particularly evident in the unskilled and semiskilled functions. Modern car factories now use robots and other technical innovations so extensively that the labor requirement is now only about thirty hours to produce a car. There were also improvements in safety for workers and a virtuous cycle was created in which cheaper products made by machines could be bought by the common man, which in turn created more demand for more production and a general increase in wealth. But that has now changed for workers in the whole of the Western world. The combined effect of getting work performed by low-cost labor overseas and the remaining work gradually being taken by computers and robots has been a steady, but now accelerating, reduction in the value of labor. And it can only get worse. Just imagine the effect of driverless vehicle technology on employment in the transportation industry. Truck driving is one of the biggest sources of employment in this country, so that could be yet another lost employment opportunity.

The message is clear: technology will be introduced at an ever-increasing rate, and its effects will be even more profound. And it's not just factory workers—skilled trades and even the professions will need to adapt and adjust. Computers and robots can now perform tasks that were previously thought to be so complicated and difficult that they would have to remain under the control of humans. Legal firms are using computers to perform work that would once have required lawyers many hours to research. The medical world is ripe for big changes too. For example, computers can scan X-rays and find tumors many times faster and more accurately that experienced oncologists. Furthermore, companies are now outsourcing technical work, such as engineering design to countries like India, where they have access to skilled and educated workforces that work at much lower rates of pay.

Everything looks quite dismal for everyone except for the lucky few who pick the right industry or get a senior position in a successful company.

2. Inequality

Inequality of income is a direct result of the wage stagnation which is hollowing out the middle class. Inequality of wealth runs along the same lines except that those who were able to buy houses and make investments years ago have oftentimes benefited from low-interest rates that inflated the value of assets.

Today's young people are the ones who are being hit the hardest, particularly the ones without a post-secondary education. But even those who want an education have a more difficult path than the one their parents had. Education costs are high, the returns are not as good as they used to be, and whatever career is chosen there might be an uncertain future. Furthermore, any investment in assets is now likely not to result in the gains that have been seen in the past because interest rates are likely going nowhere but up.

The ramifications of inequality have not been fully felt yet. It will have an ever-increasing pernicious effect on society that could eat away at the very foundations of our society. America was built on the premise of opportunity for all, and so long as a person was prepared to work hard, life could be good. Once people get the feeling that the good life is only available to a few fortunates, the political climate will change to one based on redistribution of wealth rather than the idea that wealth can be pursued through personal effort.

3. Slow Growth

The sluggish recovery has been painful and difficult to understand. With the benefit of hindsight, it should have been expected. We have been recovering from a financial collapse more similar to the Great Depression than typical post-World War II recessions, most of which were caused by excessive demand being tamped down by high interest rates and then being ignited again by lowering interest rates. This one is different. Governments and private individuals have been reducing expenditures, which has reduced demand. Interest rates cannot be lowered any more, and overseas demand has not replaced internal demand. In addition, banks have had to increase their equity and be more careful about subprime lending.

A political philosophy has emerged that is based on the concept that growth since the last recession during the Obama years must have been the result of policies put in place by the federal government. The point is made that it has never taken so long to get the economy humming again after previous recessions, and that we should now be growing our economy faster than our current anemic rate.

Some of that might be true. We could have definitely have benefited from fewer and better regulations and a more sensible tax structure, but let us not imagine that the federal government can just tinker with tax rates, business regulations etc. and expect basic trends to change. The problem is bigger than that.

The Trump tax cuts have definitely had a positive effect on growth and employment, but cutting taxes without equivalent expenditure reductions is just the old-fashioned Keynesian idea of having the government borrow money and run a deficit to get the economy moving—and the increased government expenditure just added to the stimulative effect. In addition to tax cuts the Trump administration has reduced environmental regulations by pulling back on various Obama-era EPA rules in an attempt to stimulate economic growth. While these steps have had a positive effect on the fortunes of certain industries the question remains—can we have sustained high growth with improvements in real wages without borrowing more money and making it easier for companies to produce, but at the expense of the environment?

4. Immigration
Illegal immigration is clearly a hot-button issue for many people, and understandably so. Politicians do not seem capable of making any progress on the issue. It appears to many that Democrats pander to Hispanic voters and old school Republicans

want cheap labor. People who come to this country illegally or overstay their visas are often poor and lacking in education and marketable skills. We have plenty of citizens that fall into that category already and they put a strain on our social services and economy generally. Why add to the problem? Furthermore, many who are here illegally cannot speak English, which makes it even more difficult for them to integrate and become productive members of society. It all seems like a good way to increase the size of a permanent underclass. But is it all getting worse? Up until the recent increase in asylum seekers from Central America most studies would make you think not. They showed that since 2008 the number of undocumented people was likely holding steady because the increase from Central America was offset by more Mexicans going home than staying here. Whether or not the situation is getting worse the issue should addressed logically by passing some form of immigration legislation, but emotion and grandstanding currently stand in the way of anything that would be workable in the long-term.

There are some Americans who see legal immigration as being almost as bad as illegal immigration. They see it is a process by which people of different backgrounds, often non-Christians, are allowed into the country with no regard for whether or not they will benefit the nation. Poor Hispanics might be Christians, but they compete for low-skilled work and thereby lower wages for citizens and they also fail to assimilate. On the other hand, others see immigration as a great source of vitality that counters current demographic trends and provides us with educated and dynamic people who are so badly needed in our high-tech industries.

Immigration has become something of a political football with one side pandering to increase the Latino vote and the other side wanting cheap labor while paying homage to some extreme nativist sentiments. The strongest and clearest message has recently come from Donald Trump who proved to unsuspecting politicians that it is possible to win the Presidency without courting Hispanics. Indeed, he was able to do it by actively disparaging them. Clearly the issue of immigration strikes a chord with many, but comprehensive immigration legislation still seems to be as elusive as ever.

Throughout the world, there are many examples of properly functioning immigration systems that bring great benefits to host countries, both economically and socially. On the other hand, immigration that is uncontrolled and/or badly conceived can lead to resentment and a break down in social order. In short, it is such an important and emotive subject that it needs to be addressed without delay.

5. Demographic Changes
We are participating in two big demographic changes in America. The most obvious one is that the population is becoming less white all the time. Soon the majority of Americans will be non-white because immigrants are predominately not white and those immigrants tend to have more children.

The other big change is that we are getting older. Although America is in a lot better shape than other Western countries, and in an even better position relative to nations like Russia, China, and Japan, we do face a serious problem. We are, quite simply, gaining senior citizens faster than we are adding young people. This shift in our demographic makeup causes a number of problems.

From an economic standpoint legal immigration is a net positive because it adds young people to our population who will contribute to the tax base. And immigrants, particularly those with skills are more likely to be entrepreneurs and gain higher education, so they have a net positive effect on the economy as a whole. On the other hand, it is difficult to imagine the financial benefits of having older, and generally less healthy people.

We have developed a system of paying for entitlements by taking a portion of working people's wages, and using these funds to support the elderly. Unfortunately, as the percentage of working people falls the percentage of older people increases. The fact that 13% of our population is currently over 65, but predicted to be 20% by 2050 illustrates just how fast things are changing. Current fiscal models do not work without large increases in taxes because the young working population has to support more and more old people. Furthermore, if wages continue to stagnate those taxpayers will be progressively less capable of supporting the ever-expanding numbers of seniors.

6. National Decline

Rightly or wrongly, there is a pervasive feeling amongst many Americans that the country isn't what it used to be. It is as though problems cannot be solved anymore, and although we have acted as the world's policemen for years, our allies leave the heavy lifting to us and we do not get respect in return. Even tin-pot dictators and terrorists can push us around. To add insult to injury, we have allowed our manufacturing base to wither to the extent that we cannot hang onto the jobs in industries we once dominated. Altogether it feels that other countries are getting stronger at our expense while we are getting weaker. There is a dangerous feeling amongst many that we have been taken advantage of by those in our country who we entrusted to look after us because they have either stood idly by or profited from our decline. Whatever the reason for our relative decline, it is not because we have lost the colossal advantages we have always had. Our geography, educated population, industrial know-how, legal system, infrastructure, dollar as a reserve currency, etc., collectively give us a combination of assets available to no other country in the world. We are doing well, but <u>should</u> be doing better.

Do We Really Need to Change?

Of course we need to change. After all, we can't seem to get anything right anymore: never-ending wars, slow economic growth (unless subsidized by deficits), unsustainable entitlements, wage stagnation, climate change, terrorism, international competition, gun violence, insecure employment, poor education, drug addiction, expensive health care, the decline of American prestige, government dysfunction, political divisions, wealth inequality….the list goes on. Clearly, we need to be making better decisions if we are to improve America's performance.

Should we Simply Go Back to the Way it Was?

What a seductive idea. Those of us more advanced in years can remember when things seemed better, when it was easier to find a decent job and a burger cost less than a buck. Wouldn't that be great? Well, yes and no. We need to put things into perspective. Although it is possible to point to the ways certain things were better, there has never been in a time that could have been described as perfect. There have always been problems, and the world has a long history of social commentators decrying the fact that things used to be better in the good old days.

The following analysis of the decline in the behavior of youth has been attributed to Socrates:

> *The children now love luxury; they have bad manners, contempt for authority; they show disrespect for elders and love chatter in place of exercise. Children are now tyrants, not the servants of their households. They no longer rise when elders enter the room. They contradict their parents, chatter before company, gobble up dainties at the table, cross their legs, and tyrannize their teachers.*

And in 1982 Merle Haggard expressed some real concerns for the ways thing we're going in America in his song "Are the Good Times Really Over":

> *I wish a buck was still silver*
> *It was back when the country was strong*
> *Back before Elvis, before Vietnam war came along*
> *Before the Beatles and yesterday*
> *When a man could still work and still would*
> *Is the best of the free life behind us now*
> *And are the good times really over for good?*
>
> *And are we rolling downhill like a snowball headed for hell*
> *With no kinda chance for the flag or the liberty bell?*

Wish a Ford and a Chevy
Would still last ten years like they should
Is the best of the free life behind us now
And are the good times really over for good?

I wish coke was still cola
And a joint was a bad place to be
It was back before Nixon lied to us all on T.V.
Before microwave ovens when a girl could still cook, and still would
Is the best of the free life behind us now
Are the good times really over for good?

Country singers often have a knack of recognizing society's angst, so clearly there were plenty of problems being felt back in 1982. And it makes you think that harking back to a golden age when everything was the way it should be is an illusion.

Certainly some things were better, but many aspects of life would seem intolerable today., for example:

- America's life expectancy was 47 in 1900, in part driven by the fact that about 10% of all infants died before their first birthday. Life expectancy is now almost 80 and infant mortality has been cut by more than 90%.
- The Ku Klux Klan is now a fringe group with little political power, but in the 1920s it was a mainstream organization. It was anti-Semitic, promoted the suppression of blacks, and actively worked to exclude immigrants from Catholic countries.
- The homicide rate rose to nearly 10 per 100,000 in the 1930s, then dropped after the war but rose again to more than 10 per 100,000 through the 1970s and 1990s. It is now less than 4, which is a bit better than the same as it was in the post-war period.
- There were a number of politically motivated assassinations in the 1960s: John F. Kennedy; Malcolm X; Martin Luther King, Jr.; Robert Kennedy. Thankfully, that string of assassinations has not been repeated.

- Sexism, racism, and homophobia still exist, but the situation has improved dramatically since the 1950s. The right to vote, buy and rent property, and be gainfully employed is now regarded as an equal right of all citizens, regardless of gender, race, ethnicity, religion, or sexual orientation.
- The casualties during the Korean and Vietnam Wars were far greater than the Iraq and Afghanistan conflicts.
- The Cold War was an extended period of insecurity during which a devastating nuclear war was an ever-present possibility. North Korea and the continuing terrorist threat, although serious, pale by comparison.
- Much of the post-WWII years were plagued with the fear of expensive and/or uncertain energy supplies that threatened to destroy our economy, and forced us into questionable political and military alliances. We are now energy sufficient and on the verge of being able to produce an ever-increasing percentage of our energy needs from domestic renewable sources.
- Many people consider current federal tax rates to be too high and that this is the reason for our moribund financial recovery. But the current federal tax receipts as a percentage of GDP are pretty much in line with what they have been since WWII —currently about 17% versus an average of 20.9% between 1946 and 2007. Furthermore, even before the Trump tax cuts America had the third lowest tax receipts as a percentage of GDP compared with the other countries in the Organization for Economic Cooperation and Development (OECD). Only Mexico and Chile collect less taxes.
- What about federal expenditures—are they a problem? The short answer is yes. Apart from the 1990s federal expenditures, as a percentage of GDP federal expenditures have been on a steady rise since the end of WWII. But to put this slide into context, expenditures relative to GDP are now actually lower than most of the Reagan years. The other thing to consider is that the problem might not simply be waste, fraud, and abuse. It might be that the government is doing too much, or what we are doing costs too much—like health care, for example.

Overall, things are currently not as bad as we sometimes think they are, and we haven't just fallen off a cliff, or recently taken a wrong turn. But that does not mean we should go back on auto-pilot and carry on going the way we have been. Which is basically bumbling along patching and mending and throwing money at problems to make the pain go away. But let's not panic and chase whatever sounds good in a sound-bite. We could easily make things worse if we introduce badly thought-out measures intended to get us back into an imaginary time when everything was perfect. We need to take a hard look at what is going on and come up with plans to prepare us for the future, not some bygone fictional utopia.

While our government is inefficient and unresponsive to the real needs of the nation, it might be instructive to take a step back so we can see the bigger picture. Although what goes on politically can seem irrational, it is not a great deal worse than what it was in the past and wasn't a total failure. In fact, America has been exceptionally successful, particularly when you look at what has been tried and failed in other countries. Perhaps we weren't supermen in previous years—it could be that we were just lucky to have such a good head start. Could it be that we haven't gotten worse, but that our competitors have started to catch up?

How Did We Get Here?
It is true that America has been blessed with some unparalleled advantages when it comes to geography, but it could have failed or remained a medium-sized nation on the Eastern Seaboard if the citizens and leaders had not been up to the challenge. Having bountiful land and opportunities is no guarantee of success, as can be illustrated by many nations in South America and Africa. But unlike other countries with some of the same opportunities, America's government has always been able to pursue the big things when the need arose. The government has consistently been able to tap into the mood and aspirations of the people to enable progress through a national will based on consensus. Without the popular support of the people who paid taxes it would not have been possible to: enact the Louisiana Purchase,

acquire the western United States and Alaska, wage the war in the Pacific and Europe, rebuild Europe with the Marshall Plan, or pursue the space program, etc., etc. Although these incredible advancements were facilitated by the government, it did not create the wealth necessary to pursue these big national undertakings. The necessary cash has always been created by businesses and individuals who had the freedom and the drive to pursue success.

A proactive, democratically elected government using wealth created by private citizens is now recognized as one of the reasons America became the most powerful nation on earth, but it was not always universally supported. Conservatives thought any kind of government expenditures were excessive, even when it came to expanding US territory and building vital infrastructure like the railroads. And the economic turmoil of the Great Depression turned peoples' lives upside down with effects so severe that many thought the time for liberal democracies and free-rolling capitalism was over. Some countries, notably Germany and Italy, turned to authoritarian forms of government that were thought to be the only antidote to the combination of ineffectual democracy and rampant excesses of capitalism that had destroyed so many ordinary peoples' lives. The fascist and communist parties grew into powerful political forces in many other countries in Europe as they saw what appeared to be success stories in Germany and Italy or a muscular and interventionist form of socialism.

Although the 1930s saw the rise of fascist and communist parties in America, they remained small and ineffectual. The idea of dictatorships whether right or left-wing was largely rejected by the electorate. The government, however, did alter its attitude towards business and direct assistance to people in need—what many now call socialism. Through the New Deal the government became much more interventionist than it had ever been. Money was directed to certain industries and public projects were started purely with the intent to provide jobs. Actions that would have previously been unthinkable in a country that valued free enterprise above all else. There has recently been a lot of second guessing about whether or not the New Deal was actually successful when it came to repairing the economy. But that theoretical economic stuff misses the point. These were exceptional times and the people were tired and frightened. And Europe gave us a good example of what can happen when enough people start to feel that their situation is hopeless and the government does not care.

Our success appears to have been built on individuals and businesses having the freedom to take advantage of opportunities available and a governmental system that not only allowed that to happen in a safe and orderly fashion, but also willing to step in and do what was necessary when action was beyond the capabilities of individuals and private groups. A delicate, but relatively successful balance. Although we have not recently been doing that badly by historical standards, there are some troubling trends that need to be attended to with some urgency. Although a number of those trends have been with us for quite some time they are now compounding and intensifying. Life for huge segments of our population is getting measurably worse and things could deteriorate further.

History tells us that when people suffer for too long they start to demand changes in the way wealth is distributed. If the numbers of unhappy voters are sufficient our democratic process will ensure that they are heard. The ensuing social upheaval might not be to the long-term benefit of the economy or the social fabric of our country. The first step is to define the major issues that need immediate attention.

Chapter 6

Government: Costs and Effects

Our Nation's Overhead

Calvin Coolidge famously said, "the business of America is business" and this was taken to mean that America should allow people to live their lives and conduct commerce with as little governmental interference as possible. There is, of course, an ongoing debate about what constitutes too much government, but his message was right on the money. All forms of governmental actions have the potential to skew market forces and thereby have an effect on the ability of business and society to function efficiently.

To understand the effects of government on the efficient operation of business, and indeed the well-being of society as a whole, it is instructive to draw some parallels between common business practices and how governments function.

The most obvious similarity is that both businesses and governments sell goods and services to their customers. But there are some quite profound differences. In private industry items purchased are most often bought and paid for by individuals making personal and commercially driven choices, but when it comes to the government it is voters who make spending decisions for taxpayers. Although a government's customer base is much broader and more diverse than a single company's they are both faced with the same basic challenges—how to understand and then satisfy the needs and wants of the consumer in the most efficient manner possible.

In many ways companies have a simpler job because competition provided by the free market gives them a performance report card at regular intervals. The weekly, monthly and quarterly cost reports, sales figures, etc. give up to date analyses of their success or failure to accomplish the mission of satisfying customers efficiently. It is not so easy for government. For a start the identification of the customer is difficult—who is actually paying for who's benefit? The needs and wants have to be handled through a political process that is often closer to performance theater than serious decision making so real needs are often not addressed. And some of the actions and programs by their very nature are genuinely hard to define, and long term in nature. To make it worse the lack the discipline provided by the free market tends to make meaningful assessments of actual performance difficult. It should come as no surprise that governments do not provide the same level of focused attention to performance and efficiency that we associate with private industry. And that's a problem, but the effects can be mitigated.

For the purpose of analysis the costs of running an organization that provides goods and services—whether it be a company or nation—can be split into two main elements: those concerned directly with production, typically: labor, equipment and materials, and what is commonly referred to as overhead—those costs that cannot be directly related to production, but are required to keep things running. They are the fixed costs like; marketing, accounting, R&D, senior management, human resource management, etc. that cannot be charged or attributed to a specific product or part of the work operation.

Although governments usually provide services that are more critical to personal safety and general well-being their functions can in some ways be seen as analogous to the head office of a major company. They both provide a framework of rules, regulations and services that are intended to promote consistent and productive behaviors of those tasked with production and delivery. If done successfully by companies, the employees, shareholders and customers all benefit. If a nation operates its government efficiently and effectively it is the citizens that reap the rewards.

Company Costs
When a company sells a product, whether it is a service or a manufactured item, the sale price must cover all costs and the desired profit. Successful companies spend a lot of time ensuring that productivity at the front end is maximized and overhead costs are minimized. It is always a bit of a balancing act. Cutting overhead costs always looks like a good target, but when the cutting is done too deeply morale and effectiveness can easily slide and ultimately detract from the company's ability to perform. On the other hand, it is very easy to allow overhead costs to grow until they become overly cumbersome. The negative effects of overstaffing can become even more destructive to a company than going too lean because the staff gets in each other's way leading to a bureaucratic culture in which rule-making becomes more important than speed and innovation. It's a slow death since measures of genuine effectiveness are so hard to determine. People might appear, or even actually be, working hard—but are they really producing value?

National Overhead
On a larger scale countries work in a similar manner, but with even more levels of complexity. But just like a company's head office it is not the government's job to produce—the prime function is to promote an atmosphere in which innovation and efficient production can occur. Clearly, when a Boeing airplane is manufactured in America the sale price has to reflect the production costs at the factory and the company's overhead and profit. But the price must also include a portion of the cost of social programs and any efficiency impacts of regulations imposed by the government. Social programs are financed through various taxes, which include: sales taxes, payroll burdens, personal income tax, and various business taxes. In addition, the government puts rules in place that affect production and operating costs. These rules are many and varied: health and safety regulations, environmental standards, planning permission,

etc. Collectively, government imposed taxes and regulations must be added into the production costs of that impressive new airplane.

Germany, like other advanced democracies, makes tax and regulatory decisions that broadly follow the wishes of the electorate. For example, the country has a culture of environmental awareness and the people have decided that investing in renewable energy is the right thing to do, even if it results in high electricity bills. Through the EU they have also decided to impose stringent controls on air and water pollution. The Germans have also decided to take an active role in looking after the well-being of their citizens through universal health care, unemployment insurance, housing subsidies, welfare, education, etc. Regardless of how much the programs and regulations are wanted or even needed the fact still remains—it all costs money, and someone has to pay. But it all seems quite fair. The citizens of Germany have chosen to pay for their social safety net through taxes and the increased production costs resulting from imposed standards such as health and safety and environmental standards. Taxes are a very obvious source of revenue to pay for governmental expenditures, but in most cases the cost of rule compliance or even the lack of rules is much more difficult to evaluate.

Overall Responsibility
Although nations need to pay attention to fiscal discipline, operating a complex society is not quite like a simple accounting exercise. We have a free market commercial system with our politics based on the principles of democracy, and the two are inextricably entwined—neither can survive without the other. Both the free market and government must satisfy the expectations of the electorate or there will be a search for alternatives. In other words, once there is even a perception of unfairness both institutions will be at risk.

It follows that the government must ensure an atmosphere of trust and fairness, which broadly means people get what they deserve. But, of course, achieving the goal is not simple. Although the feeling of fairness is a primary need of all humans, there is not a universal understanding of what it means. Conservatives see fairness as equality of opportunity whilst Liberals tend to look at outcomes. Conservatives point to the fact that many people raised in poor circumstances have achieved success by dint of their own efforts, so if they can do it everyone else has the opportunity to do the same. Furthermore, featherbedding everyone who exhibits difficulties will destroy the impulse to strive. Liberals do not necessarily discount the value of hard work, but point to social mobility statistics that show a person born in a disadvantaged environment is less likely to become successful than one raised in an affluent community.

So is our society actually unfair? Many in the minority communities believe they have had the cards stacked against them for many years, and now even many middle class whites are starting to think that there is a privileged class that uses the "system" to take advantage of them. So is it true that "perception is reality" as the modern idiom goes? Or are we just hearing the complaints and excuses from those who have not figured out how to grapple with reality?

If the government's role is to maintain our democracy and capitalist economy—and they will only be able to do so if there is popular support—it is clear that it must pay particular attention to:

1. Ensuring that all aspects of commerce are free, fair, and competitive, such that all citizens derive the benefits in terms of opportunity, access to employment and there is value to the customer.

2. Any and all services provided by or for the government have a defined purpose, are provided efficiently, and are available equitably.

3. Very importantly, the government should not stop there at doing what is deemed necessary. It must also be able to demonstrate that it has been able to create a level playing field —people are in fact being equitably and properly served by both commerce and government. All the legislation designed to protect employees and consumers, prevent discrimination, and pay for social programs will come to naught if significant parts of society continue to feel badly used by the system. And the effects will be pernicious—rightly or wrongly the focus will inevitably shift from taking personal responsibility to a redistribution of wealth to those who feel marginalized.

Basic Services

Contrary to what might seem obvious, some government expenditures and interference do not always result in an increased national overhead—quite the reverse. For example, certain financial regulations were put in place to ensure customers were not taken advantage of by unscrupulous or inadequate companies unable to meet their commitments. A level playing field was thereby created, which enhanced free and fair competition. America and Germany have taken very different paths to the provision of health care. Germany chose a delivery system that is primarily funded through taxes and administered by the government; whereas America is reliant on the private sector. Contrary to what you might expect, Germany provides its citizens with health care at a much lower cost than America. Healthcare costs actually put America at a big disadvantage to all other wealthy countries. It is necessary, therefore, to take a broader view of national overhead than just looking at the amount of money the government collects in taxes, and assume all regulations are counter productive. It would be better to look at the costs and potential benefits of regulations and the provision basic services, and then make rational assessments of their value. We can define basic services as those purchases that must be made by individuals and communities to support a standard of living that the society regards as acceptable: clean water, electricity, roads, education, health care, law enforcement, etc. It's a long list and every nation has to figure out how to provide it all reliably and efficiently. It's a daunting task because it includes establishing priorities and making value judgements. It has to be done carefully—cuts to services like education and policing can result in a better bottom line in the short term, but the long-term effects might be detrimental economically and socially.

Who Pays?

The costs of regulations and providing basic services have profound effects on societies. Regardless of how the costs and effects are distributed the bill ultimately goes to the producers of wealth. In the end, it must be the companies and working people who carry the load through taxation and paying more for whatever they buy. Having less money for discretionary spending has a negative effect on businesses which reduces their ability to hire more people, which in turn increases unemployment and depresses wages. But in this globalized world, there is an even greater price to pay. Competitively priced imported goods increase peoples' purchasing power, but those imports undercut local producers which can either go out of business or try to compete. For a company, increased productivity is one answer. The other is reduced wages and layoffs. Having cut their own production costs the only way companies can avoid the costs of basic services is to move all or part of their operations out of the country.

The answer to the question of who pays the costs and bears the brunt of the effects of: the government making bad choices in terms of priorities, failing to allocate resources effectively, excessive regulations, and the inefficient provision of government services becomes quite simple. Large companies can shift operations overseas, and wealthy investors can choose the best locations for their money. It is the small business and employees who cannot move and are in competition with low wage countries, and other nations that have figured out how to provide their basic services more efficiently. The bill gets paid by those with the least power to affect change.

Cost Control

As stated previously, the provision of basic services to the population of a country can be regarded as analogous to a company's overhead. In both cases their functions are accepted as necessary, but a few questions always need to be asked: is it identifying priorities logically, regulating appropriately, is there simply too much of it, and is it bloated and inefficient? If there were cutbacks, would the effects really be catastrophic or would it just force more efficiency? In America, we often don't know the answers, so the political battles tend to be based on emotional appeals to people with entrenched views, in lieu of thorough and properly considered analysis.

The big difference between a company assessing its overhead expenditures and a country evaluating its performance in providing basic services is that the company is forced to take the problem seriously, and make decisions based on facts. The acid test for private industry is, of course, survival. A company that does not address excessive overhead will eventually fail. But there are many business practices that remind even the most poorly run company that there is something that needs to be fixed. Not having cash to pay bills and the bank refusing to extend credit being just a couple of examples. There are better ways to intercept profitability issues and they can be utilized well before creditors knock on your door.

Many companies produce quarterly reports that reflect current and projected profitability. If the report shows that revenues cannot support the overhead, the CEO is forced to take action. The action may be in the form of increasing expenditures on technology, hiring or letting staff go, increasing the focus on research and development, or cutting back on fixed assets. Whatever actions are proposed, there will be an investigation completed and an action plan developed and implemented. The plan might be long-term—possibly a year or even longer. But even if that is the case, progress toward the ultimate goal will be monitored in the next quarter, so that the ultimate success or failure of the plan can be determined on the basis of actual results.

Government in America does not work that way. The problem is, of course, our democracy. Although reports reflecting the outcomes of policies are created, legislation must be enacted to change policies and direct the appropriate agencies. The bureaucracy is large and cumbersome. Government cannot rectify situations as quickly as corporations can. It might not be easy, but you have to pity the politicians. They have to be instrumental in providing the country with its basic services without taking too much money off the electorate to pay for it. They know very well that if essential services were stopped or taxes became too burdensome they would simply not be re-elected. The major political parties in America have two very different sets of priorities:

Democrats
Prioritize the provision of services even though that might raise taxes

Republicans
Prioritize low taxes and reduced regulations even though that might impact the provision of basic services

Although the opposing parties offer different approaches the results tend to be similar. In the battle for votes the parties usually end up somewhere in the middle. Democrats do not want to lose voters who would prefer lower taxes and Republicans shy away from meaningful cuts to expensive programs because they fear the loss of voters who would be hurt by the cuts. The results have been consistent over recent years—apart from a short period at the end of Clinton's presidency the federal government has always run a deficit.

For most of American history, it looks as though the federal government ran a pretty tight ship, with deficit spending only occurring at times of recession and wars. The picture looks very different starting in the 1970s because apart from a short period of fiscal rectitude in the late 1990s, there has been a trend towards continuing and bigger deficits. Apart from the effects of wars and recessions, it really doesn't seem to matter which party holds the presidency. The most recent deficit spike resulting from the 2008 financial meltdown is now over and we were returning to a more normal post-1970 deficit relative to GDP, that is until the 2018 tax cuts and increased budget.

The government has not had the discipline to police its outlays so deficit spending has been necessary to keep voters happy—or at least quiet. The government has, in effect, been its own banker, which goes for a comfortable life, but ultimately a very expensive one.

Effective Government

If we could remove the millstone of government from around our necks by cutting expenditures, we could transfer that money to businesses and employees and we would all be better off, right? Well, it's not as simple as that. There are many basic service functions that are so essential that we just could not countenance living without them.

Even at a minimum it is a long list and includes items such as:

- National defense
- Law enforcement
- Free and fair commerce
- Democratic infrastructure: election and maintenance of representative government
- Legal system and law enforcement: criminal and civil
- Education: free K-12, tertiary
- Utilities: water, sewage, power
- Food supply: safety, plentiful supply
- Transportation infrastructure: road, rail, public transit, marine docks, airports, etc.
- Communication infrastructure: cable, satellite, phone (landline and cellular)

- Emergency response: fire and EMS
- Basic scientific research
- Health care and medical research
- Old age pensions
- Environmental protection
- Health and safety at work
- Building standards
- Etc., etc.

We often take for granted just how good countries with developed economies have become at providing the essentials of civilized life. Modern societies have become so proficient that the majority of people in wealthy societies consider basic services to be a right rather than a privilege reserved for only those who can afford them. The provision of basic services is seen as so important that governments tend to either ensure that private companies provide the service or some form of government entity provides the service directly. The nature of some, but not all, of these services are such that they are not generally open to free and fair competition, so when private companies provide those services the government usually regulates the service.

Choices and Impositions

It follows that once the democratic process has decided the nature and extent of each of the basic services in terms on form and function the logical next step is to concentrate of how to achieve the deliverables in the most efficient way possible. No country is the absolute best in all areas, and a couple of examples illustrate this fact. It would appear that America is doing a good job in the area of electricity costs—it has one of the lowest $/kWh in the world, but failing miserably in the area of health care —having the distinction of highest cost and poor outcomes.

Every country in the world has to make choices regarding the provision of what it considers to be basic services to its citizens. As described earlier, German industry is required to absorb the effects of the political decision to adopt a "green" electricity generation policies. Similarly, American industry has to pay the bill for its own costly programs and regulations. America's excessive basic service costs come from neglect, inattention, collusion, and a failure to prioritize. They include:

Waste, Fraud, and Abuse
Yes, the usual suspects. You would like to think that politicians would get embarrassed talking about what they are supposedly going to do—but it never seems to happen. There are many examples of programs that use outdated and inefficient operating methods.

In an article entitled "Evaluating Federal Social Programs: Finding Out What Works and What Does Not" David B. Muhlhausen, Ph.D. hits on what is the real problem:

> *Federal social programs are rarely evaluated to determine whether they are actually accomplishing their intended purposes. As part of its obligation to spend taxpayers' dollars wisely, Congress should mandate that experimental evaluations of every federal social program be conducted. The evaluations should be large-scale, multisite studies to guard against mistakenly assuming that a program that works in one location or with one population will automatically work in other situations. Congress should place substantially less emphasis on funding evaluations based on less rigorous types of research designs, because their conclusions are much less reliable. Finally, Congress should exercise strict oversight to ensure that the evaluations are conducted and the results reported in a timely manner.*

> *The notion that public policy should be informed by social science has gained widespread acceptance. The evaluation of federal social programs, using scientific techniques, offers policymakers and the public ample opportunities to learn about the effectiveness of government programs. Despite the availability of evaluation methods, the effectiveness of federal social programs is often unknown in far too many cases. Many programs operate for decades without ever undergoing thorough scientific evaluations. With the enormous federal debt increasingly shaping policy debates in Washington, D.C., Congress should subject all federal social*

programs to rigorous evaluations to determine what works and what does not work.

The trouble is that we do not really know what works and what does not, let alone how efficiently programs are being run. How can we expect efficiency if we do not have clear objectives and performance data? Is there waste, fraud, and abuse? Sure there is, but that is just another way of saying that programs are not being managed properly—but we more or less knew that.

Inattention and Collusion

Another area of massive overspending on basic services is the one that gets next to no scrutiny. We are all forced to pay way too much for these services because the government has kept throwing money at them or stood back and allowed them to become unnecessarily costly. And in some cases grotesquely expensive and ineffective, or even destructive. These services have become inefficient and special interests have been allowed to enrich themselves at the expense of the people who pay the bill. Here are just some examples, but they are big ones:

1. The Criminal Justice System.

To be fair, the criminal justice system is now finally getting some attention. But the manner of its discovery as a major issue should give us all cause for concern. The protests and riots resulting from black youths being shot by police brought things to a head, but if it were not for the recession of 2008 it is very likely that it would all be business as usual.

The recession put a squeeze on all governments down to municipal level so in the process of figuring out where adjustments could be made, many localities figured out that too much money was being spent on arresting, convicting, and imprisoning offenders. The lack of money at state and local levels got the interest of even the most hardline "tough on crime" politicians because when it comes to balancing the books you have to do what you have to do. The demonstrations and race riots really got peoples' attention. It then got politicians to take notice, so finally the how and why of locking people up was talked about seriously.

Taking a look at a comparison between Wisconsin and Minnesota shows what can happen when there is political will. The two states provide us insight into the effects of mass incarceration because they are neighbors with similar populations, area, wealth, and culture. The numbers are shocking. Minnesota has roughly half the prison population, spends $74 per citizen compared to the $150 that each Wisconsinite has to pay every year. And the effect on crime? Overall rates are similar, but violent crime is lower in Minnesota.

Like many government actions and programs the high incarceration rate has some history. The problem started with the crack cocaine epidemic in the 1980s, which morphed into a more general "substance abuse" problem and the ever-increasing rates of violence that went into the 1990s. The war on drugs was thought to be the answer, and many stringent laws were enacted that required minimum sentences for even non-violent offenders on the periphery of drug crimes.

The government then went on auto-pilot, perpetuating a "lock them up" philosophy, even when the crime rate started falling. The criminal justice system now imprisons three times as many people as it did 30 years ago, when the crime rate was a great deal higher. District Attorneys (DAs) seem to have an incentive and means to lock more people up. They file felony charges at twice the rate that they did in the mid-1990s, and use the plea bargain process very effectively—only 5% of cases go to trial.

There are a number of constituencies that voice the opinion that the crime rate was falling because of the high incarceration rate, but that argument ignores the fact that crime was also dropping in other countries. Vocal proponents of continuing the policy of more and more prisons included: prison constructors, facility operators and prison guard unions—and they all had political clout. Is it any wonder the prison industry has grown all these years?

The numbers are staggering. America has the highest incarceration rate in the developed world, by a long way. It is about 3 1/2 times the median rate for Europe and about 66% higher than the next highest country—Russia.

The direct cost effects of incarceration are reasonably easy to calculate. On average, each man, woman, and child in America spends $250 per year to keep prisoners locked up. For a family of four that represents $1,000 per year. If we were able to get that number down to even the relatively high Canadian rate, we could save that family of four over $500 per year in prison costs. Doubtless some of that money would have to go into drug treatment and other services outside of prison, but there is plenty of scope to save massive amounts of money.

The indirect costs of our high incarceration rates are probably even more significant than the direct cost of the prisons. Some estimates go as high as $1.2 trillion dollars per year—an incredible 6% of the economy. The effects are not evenly spread. African-American and Hispanic men are over-represented in the prison population. This clearly has a devastating effect on communities with large percentages of the male population not around to participate in family life and the economy of the nation. Furthermore, when prisoners are released from jail it is very hard for them to reintegrate into society. Other effects often go unseen by those outside of the affected communities, such as the inability to maintain a stable home life.

Excessive incarceration is probably one of the most costly and socially destructive government programs we have. It is costly, exacerbates the racial divide, causes untold misery, and perpetuates an underclass that can never properly participate in society. The fact that conditions were allowed to become so extreme, and that it took so long for the nation to recognize the problem illustrates very well that there is something seriously wrong with how we manage governmental affairs. The public has a justifiable desire to be tough on crime, but this has been converted into the criminal justice disaster we have today. Insufficient funding and race-based protests should not be the prime movers of policy changes.

2. Health Care.
When the public is asked if they like the idea of the Affordable Care Act (ACA/Obamacare) before the 2016 Presidential Election the majority of people say no. But when presented with its key provisions, like affordable insurance for those with pre-existing conditions, they liked them. The public appears to want the provisions, but does not like the delivery system. Is that because it is an inherently bad way of delivering health care developed by people who "know what is best for you," or is it the rhetoric used to oppose it, capped off with silly talk of "death panels"? The ACA is undoubtedly bad legislation, and there are almost certainly better ideas than the ACA, but they were never discussed.

Indeed, where is the Republican alternative to the ACA? It is easy to imagine that there has been no plan developed because the present situation just does not make a credible alternative possible. Who would want to go into the next election proposing that 15 million people lose their current insurance and pre-existing conditions would no longer be covered? The trouble is that the fundamental issues have not been presented in an understandable manner. Much of the talk has been about freedom of choice, insurance, and who has to pay. And then about people being forced to buy insurance against their will just cloud the issue.

By and large, most people in America do not know how bad our health care system is in terms of value. But it was not always this way. According to Kaiser Health Tracker American health care costs in 1970 as a percentage of GDP were 7% which was about the same as other wealthy OECD countries. At 17.9% it is now roughly 45% more than Switzerland, which is the most expensive in Europe, but provides coverage for all Swiss citizens.

Just about every medical procedure costs more in America compared to other countries. The drug cost comparisons are even more egregious. We tend to think that medical procedure costs are affected by malpractice insurance costs and defensive medicine. None of that applies to drugs. But the price difference in drugs is even more extreme that for procedures. It appears as though Americans are shouldering most the impact of paying for drug company profits and R&D costs, and the rest of the world is getting them at something close to production cost. Prices are as high as the market will bear. Other countries do not allow this to happen. Canada, for example, protects its citizens from high prices by insisting that drugs are sold at something close to the world price

Obviously America is paying a lot for health care, but could it be that the health care here is just better? Many statistics would indicate that is not the case. For example, life expectancy lags behind other industrialized nations, and infant mortality is deplorable—America is twenty-ninth in the world. But these are just examples, and someone could point to excellence in some areas, such as certain cancer centers. What is needed is an assessment of overall performance.

Small businesses are particularly hard hit when it comes to health care. They have to spend proportionally larger amounts of management time and effort getting coverage for their employees, and when they do get it, they pay more than big companies. Ask the average small business owner in America if he or she would prefer the Canadian health care system, and the answer would likely be no. They might not like a government-run system on a personal basis, but their business would benefit from operating the way the Canadians do since it is easier and less costly. It also puts them on a more level playing field with big companies. In its campaign to attract investment, the Province of Ontario lists health care as one reason prospective businesses should locate there rather than south of the border. The argument is not based on emotion, it appeals to business pragmatism—specifically, efficiency and lower cost. "But Canadians have to pay more taxes" is an argument used by many to argue against adopting their system. Yes, they do, but it is not health care that makes the difference—the American government through its various agencies: Medicare, Medicaid, the VA, and various subsidies spends as much per person on health care as the Canadian government does. So we are already paying the taxes, or more accurately increasing the deficit to pay for it. In fact, the American government is certainly not stingy when it comes to spending on health care. It spends roughly the same amount as a percentage of GDP as most other OECD countries. The simple truth is that other OECD countries get better value because they get good quality universal health care in return for their expenditures.

The American approach is very different. The government has stood back and allowed—and in some cases encouraged—monopolies to charge whatever the patient or insurer can stand with little regard for efficiency, cost, and even actual care. A comparison between for-profit and non-profit hospitals shows that the quest for revenues often comes before medical outcomes. The American Medical Association (AMA), insurance companies, hospitals, and drug companies all do spectacularly well out their incestuous relationships with our politicians. The public, not so much.

If America could get costs down to the same as the average of three most costly countries in Europe—all with good systems and outcomes—there would be savings of $4,000 per year for every citizen in America. Imagine that—a family of four with an extra $16,000 to spend or save.

And it isn't just about people having a few extra dollars to throw around. There are some profound social consequences of exorbitant health care costs. The rich will always be able to afford babies and the poor can get Medicaid to cover costs. As with many modern day economic issues it is the middle class that suffer the most—they do not always have generous insurance coverage so they are faced with paying large portions themselves. One more reason the birth rate is declining amongst those who have always been the backbone of the country.

What is particularly sad is that there are already centers of excellent health care that operate efficiently in America—and many professionals know how costs could be reduced. Could we put the rhetoric aside and present potential plans to the public so they could evaluate outcomes and cost proposals to make informed decisions?

3. Maintenance of the Free Market
It is now widely accepted that increasing wealth and social progress can only be sustained if there is a free market based on the exchange of ideas, goods and services. To flourish to their full potential free markets require an environment based on personal and financial liberty as exemplified by the Constitution of the United States. People are free to go their own way, share opinions and seek whatever opportunities are available to them.

The American model of promoting and encouraging personal and financial freedom has certainly proven itself to be far more successful than any centrally directed society such as communism or fascism. But we should not imagine that the two societal models have always been exact polar opposites. Some communist countries allowed some private enterprises and even operated a number of their functional departments as separate profit center companies. By the same token capitalist Western societies have found it necessary to control and regulate the behavior of privately owned companies to ensure competition was genuinely free and fair. The break-up of Standard Oil and AT&T being famous early examples. Since then, the American government has introduced all manner of legislation that has the intent of protecting the consumer from unfair commercial practices such as insider trading and price fixing.

But just because we have the mechanisms to protect ourselves from a lack of genuine competition does not mean our government is doing the job adequately. The November 17th, 2018 edition of the Economist points out that many areas of our economy are showing signs of uncompetitive behavior. There are some companies and sectors that now appear to make more money as a return on capital than would be expected in a normal competitive environment. The list includes: Google, Facebook, credit cards, airlines, defense, and drug distribution. Furthermore, there are others that show signs of joining that group, including: Amazon, Netflix, food, household goods, advertising and pipelines.

Trust busters in America have traditionally concerned themselves with the welfare of the consumer, but there are other unseen effects of companies buying up the competition and becoming more dominant in their markets. Gobbling up small companies that have new products and ideas can look very much like taking out the competition, and can lead to a reduction of innovation. Big companies quite simply get to be more powerful in all aspects of operation: purchasing, politics, regulations, advertising, etc. And they can also set the standards for pay and benefits for employees. It now appears that larger companies actually depress wages, partly because they are the only game in town and also because they saddle their employees with non-compete clauses.

What to do is a difficult question, because some of these companies, particularly the new high tech ones provide good and apparently low cost services to the consumer. But just because the customer is not directly paying does not mean the service is free. The money comes from suppliers, so the bill does eventually get paid. And although some companies are working on thin margins right now it does not mean they will not take advantage of their power at a later date.

Just because our big companies make record profits does not, therefore, necessarily mean that all is well. One real test of sustainable economic health is whether or not there are genuine national productivity gains. And the numbers do not look good. If we are allowing the creation a less competitive environment with all its negative connotations we cannot avoid becoming steadily less efficient. The inevitable consequence will be a slide into being less internationally competitive, surviving only by paying our workers less.

Could it be that our government is asleep at the wheel?

Efficient Nation
As described earlier, if America were a company it would be easier to zero in on the real issues. But even then it would be difficult because we have more of an overhead rather than a production problem. Providing ourselves with the basic services we consume is costing too much.

If we seriously want to raise living standards and run a balanced budget, we have the following choices:

a) **Refine the Status Quo**
    • Cut back on services we receive and/or
    • Raise taxes to pay for what the services cost

or

b) Make Radical Changes
    • Ensure the free market system is properly functional by ensuring there is genuine competition in all areas of the economy
    • Define what constitutes a required basic service
    • Define outcomes required from each of the basic services retained
    • Assess all government regulations and evaluate them on the basis of effect and then modify as necessary
    • Institute plans for all government activities to achieve the defined outcomes and monitor to ensure success

Any rational person outside of the self-serving Washington elite and the coddled industries that buy their ability to bleed the American people would support whatever radical changes it takes to achieve success. The payoff would be huge. The indirect benefits would bring about even more dollar savings and America would be a healthier and better functioning society. Success will come not through blindly spending more on social engineering or illogical cuts to essential basic services, but by taking a business-like approach based on establishing objectives, cutting costs, and monitoring progress to ensure efficiency and value. You never know, we might even be able to restore our faith in government.

Chapter 7

Government:
Can We Do Better?

"The best argument against democracy is a five minute conversation with a voter"

— Winston S. Churchill

If you have spent any time in the Middle East or Africa you could be forgiven for thinking that one of America's greatest assets is our government. The list of what it does is almost endless—it protects our freedoms, builds and maintains our infrastructure, and ensures our safety. None of this should be taken for granted, but that is not the point. Our competition does not come from developing countries, it comes from autocratic regimes that abuse fair trade rules, and other modern industrialized nations that seem to be able to run their governments more effectively and efficiently than we do. We certainly need to ensure that we have a level playing field with the likes of China, but our main focus should be fixing our own government because it currently affects our ability to compete. And that's a big deal because the government affects just about every aspect of our lives, and it directly controls more than 35% of our economy. It seems strange that we lead the world in creating and managing profitable businesses, even though we have a government that is holding us back. It is as though we have a foot on both the gas and brake pedals at the same time.

Our American democracy is universally recognized to be one of the truly great advancements of civilization. In large part it made us who we are as a nation and also improved the lot of countless people throughout the world. That is not to say it is perfect, and the way it is currently operated certainly leaves room for improvement. It is therefore important to understand the inherent difficulties with the democratic process in order to propose improvements.

Government Function

With all this talk of small government and a "deep state" it is sometimes easy to lose sight of the purpose and function of government in a liberal democracy. As described earlier, the overall purpose of the government at its most basic level is to ensure that society operates such that its citizens are safe and that they are free to live their lives as they choose. Along the lines of "Life, Liberty and the Pursuit of Happiness". The model that has exhibited the most success to date is one based on free market capitalism working within a liberal democracy. Commerce satisfies most needs and wealth creation, and the democracy establishes rules that are a acceptable to the majority. But what is the government actually supposed to do? Well, just about anything the voters want it to do. Throughout the Western world governments operate differently from country to country, but they all have basically the same definable function. One definition of a democratic government is:

> *The mechanism by which the will of the majority of the people is recognized and then satisfied through the enactment of laws that enable the provision of the public projects and services that the majority feel cannot or should not be directly provided by private commercial entities.*

It follows that there are three distinct elements to fulfill the functions of government:

1. Recognition of the will of the majority—typically by political candidates describing what they understand to be the wants and needs of the people, and then being elected, if and when the majority agrees.

2. Enactment of laws in accordance with promises made during the election campaign.
3. Day-to-day running of the government in accordance with established laws, which naturally includes the enforcement of those laws.

Current Political Reality

Our elected representatives continue to put forward theories that explain our current malaise and present a few surefire proposals that would put things right, if only they could be elected. But therein lies a problem, our democracy was built on empowering those politicians who are capable of attracting votes. That is a good start, but it does not mean that they are the ones most capable and motivated to define the real issues in an efficient and competent manner, and it certainly does not mean that the electorate is always the best arbiter of what might constitute the best path forward. Without a clear mechanism for searching out real underlying problems we are left relying on gut instincts. Politicians are motivated to tell the electorate what they want to hear on the basis of how they feel.

Once elected, politicians are entrusted to actually make things happen, and that's a problem too. It could be that they lied during the election, but what is more likely is that they fail for less malevolent reasons. They likely painted an excessively rosy picture of what can be achieved politically only to have other elected officials—even those in the same party obstruct their goals. And it doesn't stop there. Although they have proven themselves to be capable salespeople they might not be very good when it comes to execution. They must also rely on unelected career bureaucrats to implement their policies and that can often stand in the way of meaningful changes. But we should not necessarily blame the bureaucrats themselves—they have to work within certain guidelines established over the years to avoid even the appearance of corruption and ensure the continuity of function regardless of what crazy ideas the new politician thinks will work. In the end, there are just so many excuses for failure that elected politicians are given a pass by the electorate that voted for them because they at least tried to represent us and do the right thing. They must have, after all that's what they told us.

The system works to a certain extent, but it is intrinsically flawed. It ends up being a reflection of the nation's inability to identify real problems and continues to maintain a process that cannot be held accountable in terms of goal achievement and efficiency.

Winston Churchill made a number of very profound statements during his political life and one that still rings true today is:

> *"Many forms of Government have been tried, and will be tried in this world of sin and woe. No one pretends that democracy is perfect or all-wise. Indeed, it has been said that democracy is the worst form of Government except all those other forms that have been tried from time to time."*

But Churchill was not the first person to express concerns regarding the efficacy of democracies, and no one has given the matter more serious thought than our Founding Fathers. They were acutely aware of the possibility that the majority could exercise their power to the detriment of society. Given the opportunity they could: ride roughshod over those with minority views, offer excessive governmental generosity, create demagogues, abandon logic, etc. It is evident that the Founding Fathers did give these issues a lot of incisive thinking because they instituted a number of mechanisms that have stood the test of time, such as separation of powers, the Constitution, and the Electoral College. It has worked remarkably well, but there have been problems.

Although the Founding Fathers established powerful mechanisms to avoid the worst outcomes of direct democracy, they did not create a perfect system. How could they? At the end of the day we are relying on ordinary, relatively ill-informed people to provide judgement on some weighty and complicated issues. The 19th century political scientist and historian Alexis de Tocqueville expressed a certain amount of skepticism when he considered the likelihood of optimal judgments being made by the majority, and that any decision would be suspect because it; " ...*bases its claim to rule upon number, not on rightness or excellence*"

In other words, leaving decisions to the public, like who is to be elected, should not be assumed to be the optimal decision just because the majority has spoken.

Unfortunately, we tend to get the politicians we deserve, so let's not just blame the politicians. They are working within a system that has been developed over many years and like most human institutions it serves a purpose but is far from perfect. Some of the major problems of our democracy are outlined below.

1. Pleasing Some, But Not All

Trying to serve the majority of people and keep the rest happy is not easy, and it never will be. Modern democratic governments are by their very nature adversarial because they give voice to elements of society that have opposing views. Although the wishes of the majority should to be the most powerful, there is typically some accommodation made to the views held by minority opinions. Indeed, the American form of government with its constitution, separation of powers, and procedural rules is designed to prevent the accession of tyrants and demagogues. It effectively puts in place restraints that encourage decisions to be made through compromise.

Decisions made this way tend to be workable compromises, but are they optimal from a performance perspective and do people get what they want? Probably not. It is different when decisions are not encumbered by the needs and wants of others, when we are free to make choices purely upon our own wants and needs. For example, a committed Starbucks customer might be dissatisfied if they had to buy their coffee at Dunkin' Donuts—it's the wrong atmosphere, they don't sell your favorite grande, non-fat, decaf latte made with soy milk, and where's the biscotti? Likewise, a regular Dunkin' Donuts customer thinks that buying a cup of coffee should be a relatively simple matter that does not require learning foreign sounding words. If coffee shops were established by a democratic government we would have three choices: learn Starbuckese, go basic at Dunkin' Donuts, or have some sort of hybrid. In all cases, there would be a certain segment of the population that is unhappy.

When it comes to actually running the likes of coffee shops it gets even worse for the government. In an effort to be transparent and avoid the perception of corruption, basic business decisions have to be shown to be above board. You can't pay key people more than a certain amount because there are compensation limits. Guidelines must be followed when buying services and consumables and managers are often not allowed the flexibility to make quick and appropriate decisions, such as the hiring and firing of employees, or distributing bonuses without a great deal of hoop jumping. Furthermore, governments tend to attract people willing to operate within the imposed strictures and ultimately they often get a reputation for being inefficient and unresponsive.

It is no wonder that even reasonably competent governments with the best of intentions don't please everyone and also seem to be inept and unable to develop answers that address the real problems—at least for many citizens.

2. Appeal to Emotions
The electorate has the unfortunate habit of acting like a collection of human beings. Consequently, the most effective appeals are the ones that bypass logic and go straight to our emotions. If they are cloaked in what

sounds like a logical argument, so much the better, but that is secondary. It is almost as though we act like a herd of buffalo, moving slowly and eating the green grass as we go. Then one of the herd sees something scary and different and starts to run inducing others to follow. Pretty soon, there is a stampede with no particular member of the herd knowing why it's happening. In most cases fatigue sets in and things get back to normal. But occasionally the herd encounters a cliff and things do not work out so well. Reacting emotionally and following the crowd without understanding why is not such a good idea, but like other social animals we find it hard to resist.

As described earlier in this book we all have deep-seated emotional predispositions that are based on the survival skills of our hunter-gatherer ancestors which have then been added to and refined by our own personal genetic makeup. After birth they were then molded by our social environment and experiences, particularly in early life. The deepest and most powerful emotions tend to be the ones related to survival. Mortal danger from physical attacks and denial of access to food, water, and shelter bring an immediate and visceral response in us all.

The next level of emotions can be excited by a feeling that our culture is under attack, particularly from outsiders, but also by people in our own society who are different enough to threaten our family and way of life. Those differences can be racial, ethnic, religious, or even just a variation in the way of thinking concerning how things should get done.

Learning experiences also affect the way we react to situations and occurrences by fashioning a view of the world that gets embedded into our psyche in early life which very often gets reinforced as we get older. Once attitudes and beliefs are locked in they almost never change. We are therefore primed to see the world in a particular way and respond to any situation in a pre-programmed manner. This means that we tend to search for information and arguments to support our beliefs and the decisions that we want to make. In America this usually means standing for solutions that can be seen as either liberal or conservative in nature.

A politician believing he can be elected as a Democrat will try to appeal to voters who believe social justice is of primary importance and that it can be brought about by government policies. Proposals might include taking money from the venally rich and powerful who suck more and more money from the middle class and the poor purely for their own benefit. A Republican candidate, on the other hand, will propose solutions that rely on private enterprise with little or no input from the government. It is their job to protect the country from the ever-growing numbers of illegal immigrants, lazy scroungers who do not pull their weight, and a government that wants to take money from productive people, redistribute it to the feckless, and waste the rest. For many voters, it really becomes a matter of deciding which side is closest to their core beliefs—which then becomes their identity.

We therefore know who is right or wrong before someone even presents the details of their case. It all sounds rather like a zero sum game in which there has to be winners and losers. Clearly someone is right and the other is wrong. But neither of the established party contenders would argue that they are proposing a winner and loser scenario. Democrats would argue that fairness and equity should come first because society cannot flourish without it, and if the rich have to contribute more that's OK because they will not really suffer—they can afford it. A Republican would say that protecting the economy and allowing it to grow is the priority because if it falters no one will benefit, and the poor will get even poorer. Both sides believe that their way will result in greater wealth and happiness for the majority of people.

The fact that we are all predisposed to vote in line with others in our "group" certainly brings about social discipline and stability—we know where we stand. But it does have a huge downside. If new ideas are presented by the other side or sound to be contrary to the established truth accepted by "people like us" we reject them without too much thought. Our emotional attachment to our team requires us to stick with our beliefs—anything else would be letting our side down.

Even though we have certain preset emotions that dictate our outlook on life, our emotions can also be enflamed by situations and even powerful oratory, and that has been happening in human societies for eons. Those early experimenters with democracy, the Greeks, recognized the phenomenon and had concerns. Plato and Aristotle expressed doubts that the democratic system would be functional because people could be influenced by their emotions and too readily fall prey to demagoguery.

The Greeks were right to worry, particularly when circumstances change. Our emotions can be triggered by events that appear to threaten our security, and this can be even more powerful than our pre-programmed view of how society should function. If a danger is menacing enough many deeply held notions about how to behave go out of the window. When faced with severe economic hardship people can do things that would have been regarded as unthinkable even weeks before. The loss of shelter, income, and access to food turns civilized people into survivors who will break many of the rules they previously held dear. Times of war are an extreme example of a situation affecting the way people think and behave. Populations generally come together and readily accept a limitation of personal freedoms and are happy to see the government exercising power in ways that would not be close to being acceptable in normal times. Fear is a great motivator.

Indeed, the threat of insecurity and feelings of fear have long been recognized as the best and most potent tool in any politician's arsenal of persuasive messages. Prior to being the head of the German Luftwaffe during WWII Herman Göring was a skillful politician who understood very well the ways in which people are motivated. After the war he is reputed to have said:

> *"The people can always be brought to the bidding of the leaders. That is easy. All you have to do is tell them they are being attacked and denounce the pacifists for lack of patriotism and exposing the country to danger. It works the same way in any country."*

Creating a sense of danger as a political tactic goes back to well before the 20th century. It appears that Samuel Johnson, an 18th century English writer understood the phenomenon well when he wrote in1775 that, "Jingoism is the last refuge of a scoundrel." What he meant was that excessive use of patriotism for political ends is a cheap and dishonest way to curry favor with the public because it uses the tactic of instilling both tribalism and fear of outsiders to gain support. He warned people to be wary of the politician who consistently wraps himself in the flag for he is likely devoid of logical arguments and is resorting to the manipulation of voters' deep-seated emotions.

But also be wary of the politician who sounds logical but is really making a pitch to other lower but significant emotions. The approach might not make us feel threatened or fearful, but if it is done right it is a guaranteed winner. How do we know that? We have all been led down a path paved with old ideas and clichés for years, and we keep falling for it. We are happy to accept flimsy plans that have little substance and successful politicians keep giving us what we want, but in reality it is just a message that "people like us" would like to hear.

3. Money
Money clearly influences the behavior of politicians and it is markedly so in America compared to other advanced democracies. Cold hard cash clearly buys influence, but that is only the start of the corruption. The need for fundraising also reduces the effectiveness of politicians because elections keep coming round so there is a continuous need to show up and ask for donations. It follows that wealthy people have more power than regular voters. This is an issue that is so fundamental to our democracy that we cannot leave things the way they are.

4. Electoral Districting
The size and shape of electoral districts is the responsibility of the states and often dictated by the local politicians who would benefit from how they are designed. Unfortunately, this can lead to very comfortable situations for both parties, because they give themselves safe seats. This results in a situation in which incumbents need only appeal to the party faithful—a recipe for little thought and innovation with a serving of warmed-up dogma.

5. Divided Nation
To put it politely, our political discourse is currently dysfunctional. We have endless debates regarding the relative merits of conservative and liberal philosophies and how to institute them. Unfortunately, what usually happens in our public discussions is that we each proffer solutions consistent with our own preconceived beliefs and when pressed we offer supporting arguments that "prove" that only we have the magic bullet. We rely on

the belief that it has worked before and it fits with our overall view of how society should look.

We have been raised to believe that our two-party system is the only possible way of running our democracy. That may be so, but it certainly has the downside of playing to the human tendency to pick sides and stick with them no matter what, also known as tribalism. It has been a recipe for partisanship that was thought to be detrimental to democracy, even in the time of the Founding Fathers. George Washington was not a fan of the two party idea and John Adams said:

> *"There is nothing which I dread so much as a division of the republic into two great parties, each arranged under its leader, and concerting measures in opposition to each other. This, in my humble apprehension, is to be dreaded as the greatest political evil under our Constitution."*

Strong words, and maybe somewhat prophetic.

The parties have morphed into ones now described as representing groups of ideas said to be either conservative or liberal with the biggest philosophical split coming from views concerning the intrusiveness of government—i.e., how much and what the government should spend money on. There are some who think that fiscal rectitude and small government will solve all of society's ills because the government just gets in the way personal responsibility. By the same token, there are others who believe money should be made available if there is a wrong to be righted or that society would benefit from government expenditure no matter what the cost. The reality is that both sides can put forward examples of when their approach has worked in the past. In the end, it tends to be a battle of ideologies rather than a search for cooperative ways to address the matter at hand. So what do we do?

It might a good start to recognize the fact that most people do not want either of the established parties' grab-bag of positions. Indeed, who says either party represents my views? What if I have a strong attachment to the concept of private enterprise, but believe in a woman's right to choose, or that some gun control and the right to self-protection are not mutually exclusive? And what if I believe in social justice, but do not want taxes to be excessive and have the government featherbed everyone who feels badly treated? Although we appear to be a politically divided nation there is a huge overlap in the middle when it comes to simply wanting things to work. How about seeing if there is common ground in terms of goals and only then move on to how they might be achieved?

The scope of our governments' (federal, state, and local) activities have greatly increased over the years. In the early days of the Republic the primary functions of government were national defense and maintenance of social order but that has changed fundamentally. Today the government has a much larger scope of responsibility such that it now supports, controls, and influences practically all aspects of our lives. There are clearly always wrongs to be righted, sufferings to be assuaged, and improvements to be made so it is only natural that people have a tendency to vote for more and more of just about everything thought to improve life in general.

But there has to be limits. Eighteenth-century Scottish philosopher Alexander Fraser Tytler prophetically wrote:

> *"A democracy cannot exist as a permanent form of government. It can only exist until the voters discover that they can vote themselves largesse from the public treasury. From that moment on, the majority always votes for the candidates promising the most benefits from the public*

treasury with the result that a democracy always collapses over loose fiscal policy, always followed by a dictatorship".

Rather than having our economy collapse and descend into dictatorship, it would be better to take a long hard look at the performance of our government, and then make the necessary changes.

The fact that American governmental expenditures, in all their forms, now constitute such a significant portion of our GDP is not necessarily a bad thing. Many other countries are functional and spend much more. Depending on your particular political perspective the amount we spend is either not enough, just right, or too much. It gets down to being a matter of what we really want and how much we are prepared to spend. And government influence does not stop at collecting and spending tax dollars. Government bodies also control, or at least affect, the behavior of privately held companies and individuals through regulations and laws intended to create or modify actions for the benefit of society. Banking regulations, labor laws, environmental rules, health care rules, utility regulations, urban planning, building regulations, being just a few examples.

The government has such a huge impact on our national competitiveness that it makes sense to take a serious look at its performance from top to bottom. When this matter is discussed the argument usually centers around the amount of tax dollars we are spending, but that might not be the best criterion to judge whether or not it is the best use of resources. The real issue is value—are we getting the results we want in a cost efficient manner? Misallocation of resources, wasteful spending, and other inefficiencies are just symptoms—they do not cause the problem. The root of the problem is the way we elect politicians and hold them accountable.

Unfortunately, as with addressing so many other problems in our lives, the solution starts with all of us taking a good hard look in the mirror. It's time to stop complaining about how partisan we have become, how useless Congress is, why we need a different President, etc., and take personal responsibility for ourselves and our country. It might make us feel comfortable watching our brand of news and political messaging on cable TV, but in our hearts we know that the other side is unlikely to be any more stupid or uninformed than the members of our team. Maybe they just have different opinions, for possibly good reasons. It is time to set aside emotionally driven preset attitudes and engage the logical side of our brains. Only then will we be able to identify our nation's problems and priorities. The next step is to agree on desired outcomes and only then adopt the most appropriate strategy.

The good news is that the vast majority of people want more or less the same results. Good education for our kids, good jobs, affordable health care, safe streets, etc. As humans, we are not destined to be controlled by partisanship alone—we have the ability to think things through, agree on common goals, and then cooperate.

Can we do it? You bet we can, but it will require a major rethink about how we operate our democracy.

Chapter 8

What Are Our Choices?

"May your choices reflect your hopes and not your fears"

— Nelson Mandela

There are a number of societal challenges and problems that can be addressed by well-meaning individuals acting collectively. But others cannot be reliably or fairly addressed by private groups. To take care of these types of issues there must be a concerted effort by society as a whole acting through processes consistent with democracy. But we have already seen that our government, and in particular our present political system, has not been up to the task for years. It's particularly bad now, and the future looks even bleaker. Currently, it appears that we can join one of three groups who believe that:

A. The government will always be a problem, so the only logical answer is to limit its size thereby mitigating its damage to society; or
B. The government can eventually be improved, but even if that is not possible the inefficiencies and misdirected resources inherent in big government are worth the cost if we are to make society better; or
C. A populist approach that adopts the good and bad parts of the established parties' platforms that will direct us away from rigid ideology and institute the wishes of the majority.

Extreme small government and big government approaches both seem like unacceptable solutions to the American people. The third option has a great deal of merit, and much of it is consistent with Donald Trump's proposition during the 2016 presidential election.

A. Small Government

The idea that we can cut back on government expenditures and life will go on and even improve has a certain ring to it. The proposition is that the portion of the economy currently operated by the government will be redirected to private citizens so they will have control over where the money goes, not where politicians say it should. The laws of supply and demand will solve all the problems of excessive costs and ensure that there will be sufficient products and services so all citizens will have access to everything they really need.

There are a few big problems with this approach when taken to the extreme. Making the government smaller involves cutting federal expenditures. Discretionary spending as a percentage of GDP is at an all-time low by modern standards, so any serious dent in the federal budget will have to come from the likes of Social Security, health care subsidies (Medicare, Medicaid, etc.), and defense.

Therein lies a problem. Social Security currently represents the total income for 40% of the retired population and constitutes an important source of retirement income for many more. You could take the position that if there were no Social Security, those people would save more for retirement and the problem would be solved. The same with Medicare—save enough for medical treatment and you will be OK. But is that realistic? And Medicaid —if poor people without health insurance were to just try harder to get a better job with medical coverage or they put money aside for medical treatment they would everything be fine? History would say "no." The introduction of Social Security, Medicare, and Medicaid were all introduced to relieve some serious social problems like hunger and premature death.

Imagine that a couple is saving enough money for retirement so they can pay for living expenses and health care. Let's assume that they are prepared to live modestly and one has a semi-serious long-term illness. Assuming they need $35,000 for living expenses and $18,000 for medical, making a total of $53,000. Many financial advisors tell us that yearly withdrawals from a retirement nest egg must be 3% up to a maximum of 5% per year if going broke is to be avoided. Even at the maximum withdrawal rate of 5% this requires our couple to have saved $1,060,000 by the time they retire. This might have been a tall order for people earning and saving since the 1970s, but in today's workplace environment with lower wages and unreliable employment it is plainly an unfeasible plan for the future.

The problems with not paying for Medicaid are even more obvious. Someone earning twice the minimum wage and trying to bring up a family cannot possibly afford full-priced medical care. Let alone the problem of saving enough for living expenses after retirement.

The small government plan would also have to take a run at "waste, fraud, and abuse" in the discretionary part of the budget. A good idea, but it's hard. There is always a tendency to cut budgets and let the bureaucrats adjust to the lowered income. Sounds good, but what usually happens is that cuts are made to capital expenditures, which results in long-term impacts to performance. There is also a tendency to lay off staff on the service side which makes the department less responsive. Critical infrastructure and service generally get progressively worse until the public squeals and the next government restores the budget through deficit spending.

Another area of government expenditure that can be threatened by a wholesale reduction is government investment in science, medicine, and technology. A common assertion by small government proponents is that the government never created a job. The truth is that the American government has been incredibly successful at fostering innovation that has saved lives and contributed to much of America's economic success. It is easy to take our modern world with all its hi-tech gadgets provided by private companies and think that the likes of Apple, Facebook, and Amazon are nimble entrepreneurs that would be even more successful if only the government would get out of the way. While no one would deny that these companies reshaped the modern world through technical and business innovations, the truth is that they would have nothing to develop and sell if the US government had not made early investments in the development of semi-conductors, the internet, voice and face recognition, artificial intelligence, and GPS. But that is just a short list of the government's successful investments over the years.

We have all heard of successful technological spin-offs from the likes of the space program such as Teflon, memory foam, freeze-dried food, and space blankets. But these are just the tip of the iceberg. By some counts, there have been more than a thousand government-funded technologies that have eventually become mainstream products, or even the start of new industries. The following is a partial list:

• Optical digital recording technology behind all music, video, and data storage
• Fluorescent lights
• Communications and observation satellites
• Jet engines
• Directional boring for oil
• Advanced batteries now used in electric cars
• Modern water purification techniques
• Supercomputers
• Digital communications
• Lasers
• Nanotechnology
• Biotechnology and new drugs
• Heart monitors
• Solar panels
• Human Genome Project

- Etc., etc.

The list of products resulting from government investment in hi-tech programs is impressive by any standard, but the education and experience gained by people actually doing the work is probably even more important. There are many examples of people working on government-funded programs going on to be key players in new companies. Indeed, without intimate knowledge of the new technologies it is difficult to imagine how our new industries and companies, like Google, could have gotten off the ground.

Downsizing government expenditure and reducing its role in society is surely a laudable goal. Personal responsibility should be the cornerstone of our society, and excessive spending distorts our economy and makes it less efficient. But it should not be done by just slashing budgets. If social programs are simply cut, there will almost certainly be real pain, suffering, and a reinforcement of the trend towards inequality. Over time, society will become more stratified with resentment eventually leading to a political quest for redistribution of wealth. If the cuts are too big and seen as unfair, the quest for small government will result in the exact opposite as the dispossessed vote for what they see as their share of the country's wealth. Similarly, cuts to government investments in basic research and hi-tech ventures would have a crippling effect on our future as a leader in technology and the creation of new companies that can compete in the world economy. Our major future competitor, China, has made some rational decisions about future industries and they are pouring huge amounts of money into their early stage development. If we give them a head start it will be hard to catch up.

B. Money For All
There are many who hold the view that small government proponents are uncaring, selfish, and out of touch with the needs and wants of ordinary folks. They believe that government involvement keeps society civilized.

One only has to look back to the situation a hundred years or so ago to see that government expenditure directed towards the needs of society can bring about tremendous benefits to the entire population. Tax-based public education produced literate adults who contributed greatly to the knowledge and capabilities of the workforce as demand for increased technical and literary skills expanded. Municipalities then entered other areas of social improvement and began to construct or facilitate sewers, gas lines, power production, and connect homes and businesses with telephone lines. They also got involved with public health projects like housing improvements, immunizations, and sanitary services which greatly improved the well-being of the population. But it did not stop there. The construction of roads, railways, ports, and public infrastructure were generally an essential element in the growth of the nation into the world's pre-eminent industrial power.

Since those early days, the government in its various forms has stepped in to replace the support previously provided to the poor and unfortunate by relatives and charities. Clearly there are benefits to this approach. Even in 19th century England it was understood that relying on relations and private charities was somewhat hit and miss, so they instituted a system known as "work houses" to provide minimal food and shelter to the destitute. There were many people who did not have wealthy or generous relations and who could not find charities capable of providing food and shelter. The Victorians were certainly not famous for being overly empathetic, but they were fairly rational. They came to the conclusion that compared to charities, the government was in a better position to make more rational and consistent decisions with regard to who gets what help and for how long.

The concept that the government can and should step in to support each and every service and person is, on the surface, quite beguiling. After all, if there is a demonstrable need and the community is capable of fulfilling that need why not turn to the public purse?

While everyday experiences resulting from this sort of approach can feel benign or even quite pleasant, the long-term effects can be devastating as more and more resources are redirected away from innovation and wealth production and towards any group that feels uncomfortable, abused, or simply not sufficiently motivated to work. Taken to the extreme, throwing money at everyone who asks for it just does not work. There are no black and white answers, so judgment and reasonableness have to be employed—and that is far from easy.

C. The Populist

For those of us who could get past some of his more extreme and controversial rhetoric during the run up to the 2016 presidential election, Donald Trump offered something new and refreshing when it came to governing the country. But let's be clear, getting past some of his messages was not easy: Mexico paying for the wall, banning all Muslims, and contending that hardly anyone in our government is competent. Also, stating that practically all of our problems have been brought about by others, foreign and domestic, who have been robbing, cheating, damaging, and taking advantage of us. All in all, a grab-bag of over-the-top rhetoric.

But there was some good messaging, too. He eschewed standard Democratic and even Republican dogma and was still able to get the Republican nomination. Trump campaigned on keeping necessary government programs like Medicare, Medicaid, and Social Security; reducing regulations on businesses; and using his business acumen to make government more effective. He was also prepared to be more aggressive when it came to trade deals with foreign countries and encourage American companies to keep jobs at home.

What was particularly exciting was that people no longer had to choose between the tired old left and right messages which have consistently been proven to be unsuccessful. The electorate could now choose to retain the essential social fabric that kept ordinary people out of poverty; have a lean government that would be run efficiently; and work proactively for American workers instead of special interests, illegal immigrants, and those who did not want to work. Although none of the political pundits knew it at the time, Donald Trump sold a message that America had been waiting for.

But of course we all now know what happened. Like all good salesmen he was able to identify his customers' wants, needs, and fears, and then fashion a campaign that would satisfy those needs. Donald Trump clearly had all the skills to sell his message, but once inaugurated it became obvious very quickly that he lacked the management and leadership skills to make it all happen.

The Choices

We are, therefore, faced with some rather unpalatable choices:

- Go for Small Government and risk losing decent health care and pensions for millions; damage our competitiveness by reducing expenditure on infrastructure, essential basic research, and beneficial hi-tech programs, etc.; and exacerbate inequality which will eventually lead to a populist backlash ultimately resulting in a more socialist country.
- Go for a Money For All approach which will change the country from one based on self-reliance and opportunity into one that caters to the people who whine and cry the loudest; hobbling innovation, business creation, and growth with a shortage of people and investors willing to take risks. Why would you? The government is providing a featherbed alternative and that is way too comfortable.
- Wait for a new political messiah who can carry the message of small, but essential government that cuts across party lines, and then actually follow through and make it happen. After the Donald Trump experience, it could be that it will be a long wait. Many people have been so traumatized by the Trump administration that they will likely be scared of anything that sounds new and different, so they will return

to their old party pablum—after all, it feels safe and comfortable.

Whichever political persuasion is favored, it should be understood that government intervention costs money to administer, pulls resources from other potentially productive areas of the economy, and alters what would have happened under a free market system. All forms of government intervention should, therefore, be treated with great suspicion.

D. Pragmatic and Cost Effective Government

While both established parties would like to project an image of wanting just the right amount of efficient government, we really know that both of them have their own particular axe to grind. The Republicans are pro-business and smaller government and profess a desire to refrain from wealth distribution and social programs. The Democrats are more likely to side with the underdog and appear to be open to creating or expanding government programs if they feel that it will be good for society.

The trouble is that neither party has been able to deliver the goods as promised. And that is not a particularly partisan thing. In recent years, Congress as a whole is typically getting an approval rating of somewhere between 10% and 20%. Based on performance, you would ask yourself why they would deserve anything better. The trouble is that no side seems better than the other. The economic numbers and measures of social well-being do not seem to change that much regardless of who controls the House of Representatives, the Senate, or even the Presidency. The one exception in modern times appears to have been the Clinton years. Not only did the economy perform well, there was a federal surplus and even significant improvements to the lives of the less well off. That was a time when we had a Democratic president and both the House and Senate were controlled by Republicans. Is that the guaranteed path to success? Probably not. It was a time when a dot-com buoyant economy came together with a president who was open to dealing with the opposition. Maybe it was just an anomaly, and surely anyone can make it look easy when the economy is going well. Real success will only come when we can figure out how to make it all work in good times and bad times.

If we just look at what has been tried to date there does not appear to be much in the way of good choices. For years we have been alternating between the first two options and recently had experience with the third. And that is not good news—if we can't come up with better choices we will just have to bumble along with the present system. That means we will continue to pay more and more for essential services, and our quality of life will steadily deteriorate—under the watchful eye of our politicians.

So what are we to do?

Chapter 9

What In The World Does Work?

Is there anything to be learned from nature and evolution that can be applied to our society, thereby enhancing our long-term well-being?

Although a serious situational analysis requires a long and sober look at what is going wrong, it usually ends up being a search for guilty parties and apportionment of blame. People are often identified with certain negative human characteristics such as greed, selfishness, laziness, etc.; slotted into groups; and then seen as the opposition or even the enemy. We then try to establish social mechanisms to deal with them, which eventually become entrenched and ultimately lead to an adversarial situation.

A more positive approach would be to search for what consistently works and play to our strengths, but that too can degenerate into picking sides since the search for social mechanisms that work often identifies the merits of opposing political doctrines. You would think that an analysis based on research, experience, and logic would be the answer. That certainly helps, yet it almost always still includes some personal bias.

Whether we look for negatives to suppress or positives to encourage, it is always particularly gratifying if the evidentiary list supports our existing beliefs. Since turning over rocks and finding confirmation of what we already believe is such a pleasant experience, we do a lot of it and end up maintaining our world view. And why wouldn't we? We keep returning to the same old problem—we are just humans.

Getting Back to Basics

Perhaps we should start by putting our understanding of politics to the side for a moment and go back to the basics. Let's take a step back......way back, and forget for a moment that we are sophisticated humans with complex social problems and ask, "What in the world <u>always</u> works?"

Could the life forces of nature give us some guidance on how to develop societal strategies that will ensure that we not only survive but prosper in this fast-changing world? They might give us some clues. After all, if there were ever an object lesson on how to react successfully to rapid and fundamental changes it would be life on earth.

Without the aid of organized political parties and religions, plants and animals have developed multiple strategies to survive in just about every nook and cranny on Earth. Environmental conditions not only vary over space, but also time. For millions of years a given species would adapt to an environment and really get on top of its game. But then things would change. It would alternately get hotter, colder, wetter, drier, more or less acidic. To make matters even worse, new predators would arrive and competitors would compete for available food sources. Bad news for any species unable to adapt.

Species have come and gone, but life has never ceased to exist. Wherever there was a void, some life form would eventually step in and survive by adapting to the environment. Species had to be very good at one specific thing or be capable generalists. Some would remain in one location and others would spread out. Both strategies work, but not all the time. Staying put works until an environmental change occurs, and moving works well, providing the new place is at least as good as the one left behind. In short, nature has ensured that our planet has been covered by life in one form or another, but not the same one all the time.

The variety of survival strategies is almost impossible to comprehend. But all forms of life have certain things in common, they consume nutrients, survive predation in sufficient numbers, and reproduce. They also do something else that is less obvious—the very act of living contributes directly to the well-being of other life forms. The interdependency of flower-producing plants and insects is well known, as is reliance of fruit producing plants on birds to spread their seed. But some of the inter-species relationships appear to be involuntary, such as animals carrying some sort of parasite around with them, like insects and tapeworms. Even we super clean humans carry bacteria all over our bodies and we have more bacteria in our gut than there are cells that compose our bodies. Although the bacteria perform essential digestive duties, by a simple mathematical estimation, it is the bacteria that use us, rather than the other way round. It all seems like a well-organized merry-go-round where every living thing was put there to help another, but it really isn't like that.

There was never a plan to make it thus, and there is not an ounce of intended altruism anywhere. Whether you are a tree, grass, rabbit, bacteria, virus, or human being there is something out there that wants to consume you and the waste you produce. It is the continual search for the next meal while making sure you are not on something else's menu that keeps everyone alert and healthy—but not forever. No species was ever given the right to last forever. It has been calculated that something like 98% of all species that have ever existed are now extinct. Some were sidelined by climate change and others could not compete with newer better models. Whatever the reason, they were the losers and every living thing we see today is here because it has adapted to changes in the environment. It has been a long hard road, and in some ways it is getting rockier. Life will go on, but it might not necessarily be yours or mine.

For the sake of simplicity and to avoid theological arguments, let's say that nature started with bacteria, then simple single-celled organisms, and eventually to multi-celled plants and animals that reproduce sexually. This seemingly illogical and incredibly complex process yielded some surprising results and enabled life forms to steadily improve capabilities through the process that we call evolution. Sexual reproduction has been adopted by all the higher life forms because it appears to be a uniquely capable way of weeding out poor genetic messages and encouraging successful ones.

In its simplest form, plants and animals reproduce sexually by surviving to maturity with males being able to produce pollen/ sperm and females producing eggs which are then brought together during fertilization. This method is common when both male and female are physically static such as trees, or there is little or no opportunity to choose a mate. For example, many fish just produce millions of eggs and clouds of sperm, with no attempt to be choosy. But there is a better way. Whenever possible, nature seems to favor some sort of selective process that goes beyond random sperm and eggs coming together. In most cases it is the female who acts as the primary gatekeeper when it comes to protecting the gene pool. She very often refuses to mate unless a potential suitor can demonstrate that he has not only been able to survive, but also has strong enough genes to be able to grow huge antlers, fight off competitors, or afford an expensive car. It all makes sense if the goal is to strengthen the genes of the species—a female does not want to waste her time, energy, and eggs on a weak strain that might result in the species dying out

In the process of sexual reproduction, both the male and female of a particular species might appear to be identical to their respective fathers and mothers. However, they are able to pass on multiple variations of their genes to their progeny since each parent passes on 50% of their DNA. Each individual, therefore, possesses a slightly different genetic makeup from even that of their siblings. The gene selection is random, which means that they might be beneficial or detrimental to the survival of the offspring. In the unforgiving natural environment the beneficial genes are likely to be rewarded by survival and the detrimental ones tend to result in death, which would typically be an end to that particular genetic experiment. Nature does not care who are the winners and losers, but over time a surviving species inevitably becomes stronger and more successful. For example, turtles on the Galápagos Islands that lived at higher elevations had longer necks than those closer to the ocean because they had to feed off higher vegetation. You could assume that over the years shorter necked turtles either died or moved down the hill in search of food they could reach—either way the long- and short-necked turtles are now genetically different subspecies, each adapted to their own environment.

But turtles, like many other animals, are really just an aggregation of individuals largely ignoring each other until the time to breed. This is clearly a successful strategy of survival, but nature had another experiment up its sleeve involving creatures benefiting from the presence of others of the same species. Being in a herd offers members the advantage of having multiple eyes looking for predators, so they can collectively be aware of danger and thereby escape, or possibly take group action against the attacker. But then some animals took it a step further and acted as a group toward a common purpose, which is an even more complex behavior since each member of the group has to understand a common plan and act in a disciplined manner. In many ways this ended up being the most successful strategy nature has produced to date, and it ultimately led to Homo sapiens. Some might argue that other species have been more successful in terms of numbers, but it is only humans who are able to alter their environment, choose where and how to live, and write books.

Lessons From Nature
The vibrancy and sheer numbers of life forms on earth prove that natural evolution has worked extremely well. The process of random genetic mutations and then subsequent allowance of successful genes to be passed on to the next generation is akin to the business processes of product development and quality management. However, while such processes are simple in concept they can be mind-numbingly complex in the details of execution. We will likely never be able to comprehend the actual

workings of nature at the molecular level, but how about the basic driving principles?

Is there anything to be learned from nature and evolution that can be applied to our society, thereby enhancing our long-term well-being? The answer is an unqualified "yes," because nature gives us a road map of how to prosper in a changing and competitive world.

Advancements in societies can occur in a manner very similar to the genetic improvements of a species in nature, if they are allowed to do so. In both cases, changes are imperceptible on an everyday basis or even year by year, but changes do occur even in what seem like stable conditions. The most obvious commonality between natural evolution and societal advancement is that changes ultimately have to be beneficial. If the changes are sufficiently detrimental to the species or society they will eventually die out. In both cases the acid test is quite simple— improve or die. Only species with strong genes and societies with good working strategies survive and prosper.

The study of human history and archeology has shown us that Homo sapiens is a very durable species, but its various social structures have come and gone time and time again. It is evident that a given human society will atrophy and possibly disappear over time if the driving principles of evolution are not in place and able to function. So what are the principles that enable societies to adapt to changing circumstances and thereby remain viable and competitive?

1. Random Variations
It is clear that the production of random variations is the key to improvement and adaptation in the natural world, and it would appear that the same rule applies to the success of human societies. A look back at history gives us many examples of groups of people who have been happy to keep doing the same old thing, and many others that have actively enforced adherence to behaviors because they were proven to

be successful at one time or they were well-suited to those in power. In all cases, these groups have been left behind culturally and economically, absorbed, or quite simply died away. New ideas in human societies are in many ways analogous to genetic variations in the natural world because without them societies make no progress and are vulnerable to all manner of dangers when conditions change.

Static unchanging societies have always been the losers. Up to the 1500s, China was roughly on par with Europe in terms of wealth and cultural advancement, but they then made a fateful decision. They decided that theirs was a society that could not possibly be improved by the input of foreigners so they walled themselves off and stopped large seagoing trade. From then on they became stuck doing the same things while European cultures changed. It was always the travelers and traders who have met with success. Even in pre-history, archeological evidence demonstrates that people valued objects from distant places. It is hard to believe that cultural exchanges did not occur along with the movement of goods. By their very nature early empires involved interaction with other peoples and that cannot happen without some sort of influence going both ways. For example, after many years of conflict and persecution, even the mighty and self-confident Romans upended their pagan ways and became Christians. In more modern times it was the open trading nations of Europe that embraced innovation and change and eventually become the wealthiest. They did not achieve success by tilling the land the same way their forebears had done for centuries, they went outside their borders and mixed with others who did things differently. As you might expect, people from other areas sometimes had better ideas. The rewards went beyond new markets, raw materials, and all manner of unknown objects that could be imported. It fostered a pragmatic and entrepreneurial atmosphere that gathered momentum which eventually ushered in the Industrial Age.

Trade and overseas adventures brought many new ideas to Europe and printing technology sped things up. The history of Scotland provides an excellent example of how societies can accept new ideas and then make unbelievable progress. They ended up influencing the entire world and it all happened in a way that could not have been anticipated. As with unpredictable genetic changes in nature, an idea was introduced and no one could have predicted its impact. It changed Scotland from being the most economically poor and culturally backward country in Europe into an industrial powerhouse and a center of modern philosophical thinking.

As described in Arthur Herman's excellent book, *"How the Scots Invented the Modern World,"* it was the desire to rethink religion, move away from the Catholic Church, and embrace Protestantism that propelled the Scottish to become one of the preeminent players on the world stage. The change was not easy, because rethinking something so fundamental to life as religion requires some deep thinking and a whole lot of motivation. And the proponents had a hard sell. Scottish Protestants were a pretty dour bunch of people—they did not think too highly of any worldly pleasure outside of working, but they did have one concept that appealed to those considering leaving the Catholic Church. That concept was direct communion with God, rather than through popes, bishops, and priests. This was an attractive proposition for a lot of people because the Catholic Church of the day was widely seen as corrupt and self-serving. But there was a big problem. The word of God came from the Bible, not paid priests, and the majority of people could not read. The answer was a publicly funded education system so that individuals could read the Bible and then have an honest relationship with God, rather than the somewhat flexible dialogue through a priest in which forgiveness could be gained by professed contrition or payment.

Literacy, however, had one effect that the leaders of the church probably did not properly foresee. Once people were literate, they gained a thirst for reading all sorts of materials other than the Bible. This became an unstoppable force and Scotland quickly became the country with the most public libraries and highest literacy rates in the world. The Scottish people then went on to form debating societies and universities, producing some of the foremost philosophers of the time. One of the most influential economic thinkers and proponents of free markets, Adam Smith, wrote *"The Wealth of Nations."* It became required reading for practically all educated people in other countries—particularly in the English-speaking world. The Scottish Enlightenment was exported to England and then to America, encouraging a rapid movement toward education, critical thinking, and science. A number of educational establishments were either started or run by Scots, including Princeton University. Scots also had a profound effect in the business world. Scottish immigrants to America became very successful—Andrew Carnegie being but one example. It is a fascinating story and illustrates what can happen when people pick up new ideas and then have the courage to run with them.

Just like different genetic messages in nature, new ideas in our society can feel scary and dangerous, but we must give them room to breathe. Failure to do so will result in being left behind and unable to compete in whatever new environment exists in the future. All the millions of extinct life forms that once occupied this world illustrate very clearly what happens to those who cannot or will not change.

2. Cooperation and Organization

Cooperation between individual animals becomes more and more important in higher forms of life, particularly when their shared objectives are complex. Herd animals help each other stay safe by keeping an eye open for danger. That means that while one animal is eating or daydreaming there are likely many other eyes on the lookout for predators and when one is spotted they can all make a run for it and confuse the pursuer or harass the would-be assassin. These collective actions have been developed over the eons and proven to be a successful strategy for many species. But sometimes groups of animals need to do something more complicated. Predators, such as wolves and lions, have to understand a plan and then execute it in concert. There are likely many lessons to be learned as a pack gets better at locating and killing prey, but none of that would be possible without the ability and desire to identify a common goal and carry out a plan. It is clear that having organizational skills and then cooperating is a winning strategy for animals, particularly when the objectives are complex and dynamic.

Humans initially became expert at cooperating so they could meet the basic needs of their hunter-gatherer groups. Over time, we steadily developed more complex ways of cooperating such as having the ability to own property in agrarian and then industrial societies. The prosperity many of us currently enjoy has been achieved through many years of cooperation that has continuously improved society by making it safer, fairer, and more efficient.

Individual intelligence, hard work, and honesty are all very well and good, but in order to realize human potential a social infrastructure must be first established. A girl born in the middle of Sub-Saharan Africa will likely not achieve the same levels of prosperity and independence as the same person born in Kansas, for example.

3. Continuous Improvement, Competition, and Rewards

Plants and animals survive by their ability to take on the capricious whims of nature. Any changes in the environment can only be met and responded to with the abilities that these plants and animals already possess. That would suggest that they are passive, just relying on the capabilities nature has bestowed upon them. But it isn't quite like that. The way they survive as a species is by continuously competing with <u>each other</u> to ensure only the most worthy and strong are allowed to pass on their genetic message. Only after the battle with others of the same species is won can their next generation successfully take on the rigors of the outside world.

There are diverse ways in which a species can exert influence on the quality of the genetic message that gets passed onto the next generation. For example, female animals often refuse to mate with weak males in a manner that appears to be a conscious decision to reject unsuccessful genetic messages. But a female dung beetle is clearly not making an intellectual decision when she searches out a mate with an impressive horn. The horn's primary purpose is not offensive, it is to attract females. It seems illogical, but the male beetle has to divert hard-won nutrients into an appendage that has no purpose other than attracting a mate. You would think that his time and energy would be better spent searching out food or defending himself against predators, but that is not the case. Much of his life is dedicated to competing with other males of the same species. Dung beetles demonstrate the principle, but there are many other examples in nature of the same sort of behavior.

Although they are much more complex, herd animals like elk act rather like the dung beetle. There is competition between males to grow larger antlers and demonstrate power through physical size and strength. They have even been seen to urinate on themselves so that they look darker and therefore bigger. But it is not all appearance—once he gets a shot of testosterone and the rut sets in the male elk changes from being just another easygoing member of the herd to a rampaging bull that is totally committed to breeding with as many females as possible, and seeing off any other males that have the same idea. It is really quite a brutal and unforgiving affair. Although it appears that the male is king of the hill, the process does not treat him kindly. He does not have the healthiest of lifestyles. Being continuously stressed, getting knocked about, and eating poorly takes its toll. Female elk typically live a year longer than males in the same herd.

Nature does not care that the poor old male has a tough existence, all that matters is that he has served his purpose. He has, through competition with his peers, passed on the strongest generational message that was available.

Humans are children of nature too, and the same rules apply. While many animals compete only when it is the breeding season humans have a built-in desire to compete whenever the opportunity arises, and that is what you would expect when it is breeding season all year round. Although the imperative of individual humans is not that much different from other creatures, to ensure it is their genes that are the ones to survive, it is somewhat more complex since humans are the most social animals on the planet.

Human males became bigger and stronger than females to facilitate hunting and protect the family from outsiders. But they did so also for the same reasons that male elk grow antlers and larger, to compete with other males and earn the right to breed. As you would expect with humans, it got much more complex than boys and men fighting each other and then claiming a mate. In order to demonstrate worthiness a male had to prove his ability to look after the family unit, which meant that other characteristics like reliability, caring, and planning came into the mix. But it was not all about the family unit. As societies became bigger and more complex it became necessary for humans to act in a manner that would be beneficial to the group as a whole.

It is clear that the strict rules of evolution dictated that societies and human brains evolved in unison. Since humans owe their existence to cooperating in a social environment, they needed to be part of a functioning group; and by the same token a group could only exist if its members played their parts. For example, it follows that a genetic message that promoted strength and aggression would be passed on but a predisposition to excessive violence would not. Successful societies have always tended towards day-to-day peacefulness, but retained the ability to be aggressive and violent should the need arise. Another example would be the human tendency to be selfish and greedy, but also display altruism when sufficiently secure. In other words, hard-wired human predispositions were developed over time to fashion a social creature that would adapt to circumstances and thereby be beneficial to the long-term health of the community.

Because we are not built to be entirely altruistic, there must have been a reward system built into every society so that beneficial actions would be encouraged. At the same time, humans must have concurrently developed a deep-seated desire to seek those rewards. It has been a winning combination ever since. Members of societies competing with each other to make a positive impact and then getting a reward is clearly a successful and sustainable system. In the early days rewards would include public approval, power, comfort, and enhanced access to members of the opposite sex. We now use money to facilitate the reward process, but motivations are not a whole lot different.

Nature has provided us with a blueprint for sustainable human improvement and we ignore it at our peril. Every society that has deviated from the continuous improvement, competition, and reward model has not prospered, and in the case of the Soviet Union, fail completely. Very often the problem is that it is difficult to identify what is actually good for the community. The Soviets did in fact recognize the value of competition and reward and used it to great success in certain areas. For example, their athletes and certain scientists were very well rewarded, and highly productive workers would be given special privileges. Those who knew how to game the system, including politicians were also well looked after. But because the system was based on central decision making driven by political goals the whole process missed one essential lesson given by nature. As with continuous genetic improvements in nature, advancements in society have to actually work for the people. Even with benign or even benevolent motivations, the ongoing decisions relative to what is beneficial for society cannot be made successfully by an inflexible central authority that fails to recognize the value of competing ideas and rewarding the successful ones.

The reason Western nations have been more successful than the centrally directed ones like the Soviet Union is that they have developed systems that identify the needs of their citizens in two important ways.

1. *Rules.* To ensure survival every society needs rules of behavior, be they elephants, wolves, or humans. Humans obviously need the most complex rules, and by and large they have been able to develop workable systems through the years. There was a time when the wealthiest landowner and the Church provided rules and enforcement. But that power structure gradually morphed into political systems with elected representatives wielding the power to set rules and enforce them—and the Church providing some moral guidance, but no coercive power. There is no perfect system in the world, but the democratic systems in Western countries are largely a reflection of the wishes of the majority of the people, and are subject to modification as society adjusts to changes in circumstances.

2. *Commerce.* Although the buying and selling of goods and services is thought of as necessary and sometimes even portrayed as trivial or detrimental, it is much more. As described elsewhere in this book, it is a basic and essential part of our lives. A free market only exists because there are people actively searching out the needs of others, fulfilling those needs, and then being rewarded for doing so. The entire process, therefore, follows the pattern established by nature, which is to have beneficial acts rewarded. The free market is such an effective system

that we sometimes forget just how well it works and how its basic honesty and pragmatism gets diffused into the fabric of our everyday lives. What we buy and sell and how we do it is a reflection of who we are as a people. After all, it tells us what we truly value. Those areas lavishly funded tend to be what we demand whilst those that languish without adequate support are a demonstration of our indifference. The good thing is that if we don't like the picture we can always change it.

For any modern society to be successful it must apply the lessons of nature which require it to perform a delicate balancing act. The rules established by government are a collection of "must dos" and "don'ts" backed up by the law. Softer behavioral rules that come from civil society are maintained by informal social pressure. The government must be flexible enough to modify rules as required, and society must be constantly vigilant to ensure the essential basics of behavior are maintained but changes are made when it is appropriate to do so.

Only by maintaining healthy rewards for those who perform political, commercial, or social acts that result in the genuine betterment of society can sustainable advancements be made.

4. Resources
Competition within a species is not confined to males competing to pass on their genes. Animals are in a continuous battle over resources, which in many cases means territory. Even cute little squirrels and hummingbirds get quite vicious when it comes to getting and maintaining their space. From an evolutionary perspective, this makes a lot of sense. A given area has a limited amount of cover and nutrients to support a particular type of plant or animal so it makes sense that only the most capable occupy that space. Once the fight is over, the loser will be forced to move away and either die or find rich pickings elsewhere. The process of

fighting over territory ensures that only the strong get to use available resources. Weaker members either die out or look for sustenance elsewhere. The species is, therefore, forced to spread out, locate other resources, and survive or even increase in number.

Humans have fought over land since time immemorial, firstly to protect hunting rights and then farmland. The imperative to maintain jurisdiction over land is similar to that of any wild animal, but human needs are more complicated. Resources for humans still include land for food, but their resource needs are much more varied. They include everything we use to make, sell, transport, and use in one way or another: mineable commodities, power, water, communications, transportation, equipment, commercial space, dwellings, labor, etc.

Fortunately, the free market provides a somewhat equitable and efficient way to give fair access to resources. It might not be perfect, but it is a lot better than fighting over what we want. Resources simply go to the highest bidder, which means that the person who wants the item the most or is best able to afford it ends up owning the item. That sounds a little rough, but from an allocation of resources perspective it works very well. If prospective buyers all have the same amount of money to spend, the person who needs it the most wins—and so he should. By the same token a wealthy person is likely to be a person who is deserving of what he has, so getting what he wants is fair too—he earned it by doing something useful and that is how he got to be wealthy.

Getting access to resources in human society, therefore, works well so long as it is part of a free market system. Things can go awry if political forces step in and consume too much on behalf of society because they might take more than the economy can bear, which will ultimately lead to inefficient use of resources and a consequent reduction in living standards. Governments will always have an important part to play in any society and should, accordingly, get sufficient resources to perform their functions responsibly. But they must be monitored closely to ensure they do not consume resources that might be better used by that part of society that operates in the free market.

5. Recognition of Success
Nature has a simple but brutal way of determining what genetic messages get passed on to the next generation by natural selection. Genes that would make the organism less likely to survive get eliminated because it will die before it can reproduce. Beautifully simple.

The same process applies to humans, but since we are social animals there is more involved. Genes that protected individual humans from disease and ensured they were physically strong enough to compete were of primary importance, but their brains also had to develop skills that enabled communal existence. Beyond those hard-wired mental adaptations that enabled cooperation, individual societies developed their own particular skills appropriate to their own environment. And just like genetically driven mental capabilities, those skills were passed on from one generation to the next. In many cases it would have been a hit and miss process with communities dying out because they chose the wrong strategy. But others hit on survival skills that worked, and as pre-humans gained in intellect, they became better at developing beneficial strategies by better predicting likely outcomes. The ability to develop and then retain good practices is the main reason humans have become the preeminent species on earth.

But let us not think it is all easy. Since time began we have been faced with difficult decisions which often involved sticking with the tried and true but occasionally giving something new a shot. And the choice is not always obvious. Just because something new worked once or twice does not mean that it will work next time.

Just because something is hard does not mean that it should be avoided. Natural evolution points us in the right direction by telling us unworkable or damaging activities should be stopped, but the mechanism of relying on the death of the genetic experimenter is horribly inefficient and time consuming. Fortunately, our intellectual capacity makes it different for us. Unlike nature, we do not always have to wait for failure or disaster, we can consciously try to see what is going on, make adjustments, and then change course.

It took nature millions of years for humankind to exist and ultimately prosper—with some very important steps along the way. For example, once our ancestors discovered that wood could be burned and used for cooking and warmth things started to gather momentum. It then took thousands of years to get to the stage at which coal could be mined and burned for steam-powered locomotives. But after that it was a mere couple of hundred years until we were able to split the atom and use sunlight to power self-driving cars. It is conscious experimentation, recognizing success, and then building on previous achievements that have brought about a rate of progress that would simply not have been possible by relying on nature's way, which is basically one of random trial and error.

It follows that societies able to recognize failures and successes as efficiently and quickly as possible—and then react—will be the most durable, competitive and successful.

6. Inheritance of Success
It must be possible for successful traits and strategies to be passed on to succeeding generations. Nature does this by passing on successful genes—societies do it by recognizing successful behaviors and then making them part of the culture. For this to happen sustainably, societies must understand and appreciate which of their behaviors have

resulted in success—oddly enough, that is not always easy, particularly in a changing environment.

7. Dependency on Others

All life on earth depends on other life forms to exist. From bacteria to human beings, we all eat something that has been produced by another living thing. Living organisms either consume the bodies of others or what they excrete. Take a look around, there is something out there trying to kill, consume, or in some way live off every living thing you see—including you. It is an endless circle with absolutely all living things taking part.

Properly functioning human societies are similar, particularly modern ones in that we are all specialized. The computer programmer buys a latte, the barista uses her mobile phone to buy new shoes, and the delivery driver delivers them—in a process that also has unseen beneficiaries like accountants, bankers, and janitors, etc. It is very difficult to do anything without commerce in one form or another getting involved. And when it does, someone benefits either financially or by getting goods and services.

Activity need not necessarily be based on physical objects being passed from one person to another. Some services like education certainly involve the building of schools, transportation of students, and the like, but the transfer of knowledge is in itself something of value. Legal advice, dissemination of news, and other transfers of information also benefit people. Even health problems can benefit someone—the entire medical industry would cease to exist if everyone were 100% healthy, so even when you are ill you provide a benefit to someone.

In essence, society works when something of value exchanges hands, which clearly works best when there is a thriving economy. That is not to say benefits cannot be had in non-commercial settings like religious, charitable, or other volunteer activities since people are benefitting from each other. The only time the system breaks down is when people stop doing anything.

It follows that societies should encourage action and movement of all kinds, because any kind of activity requires cooperation which is the lifeblood of mutual benefit and progress. A thriving economy fits the bill nicely.

8. Repeated Cycles
Evolution is not a one-time thing and it does not happen quickly. It is an iterative process with no set pattern that occurs through multiple cycles of success and failure for its effects to be realized. Rome was not built in a day.

Incorporating the Driving Principles of Evolution into Society
It might seem logical to imagine that incorporating some of the basic rules of nature into human society would be a retrograde or alarming proposition. After all, we have spent centuries trying to stop behaving like animals and impose discipline so that we can live in a civilized manner. But it is not a scary idea at all, in fact, we already do it, but sometimes in a haphazard and disorganized way.

There is, however, one aspect of our every-day lives that adopts almost all the important lessons of natural evolution. Commerce based on free markets is probably the best and most successful example of how the principles of evolution can be applied for the benefit of society.

1. Random Variations
The free market throws up seemingly random variations at an extraordinary rate. So much so that we almost fail to notice how or why it is happening. Companies are constantly on the lookout for new and different products that will appeal to customers. Although it is possible to predict what customers want on a day-to-day basis, there is always some unknown

desire just waiting to be discovered and exploited—products that fill those needs often seem to come out of nowhere. Henry Ford is reported to have been asked what his customers were looking for when he started trying to sell cars. "If I had asked people what they wanted they would have answered 'faster horses'." Innovation did not end with automobiles. Who would have imagined that a technology developed for the US military would become an indispensable tool for navigating to a new restaurant? And the idea that people would want to continuously stay in touch with others they barely know using miniature computers and cellular telephone technology could simply not have been predicted or even thought to be desirable a few years ago. Just like the genetic variations in nature, free markets constantly introduce ideas and products that often fail, but sometimes win—it is the genesis for continuous human progress.

2. Cooperation and Organization

Just like higher forms of life in the natural world, companies owe their continued existence to cooperation and organization, but they take the concept to a much higher level. It is no secret that the consistently successful companies tend to be the ones that foster disciplined behaviors that bring the best out of people. They strive to use the innate capabilities of individuals so that people with diverse skills and backgrounds can be part of teams that are much more productive than they would be independently or acting in a disorganized manner. Companies that fail to function using cooperative and organized teams are destined to fail.

3. Continuous Improvement, Competition, and Rewards

The free market is the ideal driver of continuous improvement because it will not tolerate a commercial enterprise that rejects the concept of improving their product or business model. Competition is the taskmaster that constantly reminds companies that they must keep up or be left behind. The rewards of continuous improvement can be mere survival, but can also be tremendous wealth for employees and shareholders alike when a position of industry leadership is attained.

4. Resources

When companies compete for resources the free market does something remarkably similar to territorial animals competing for feeding and nesting space. Only healthy and successful companies can afford the best spaces such as physical retail outlets or even a digital presence. But business is more complicated than just having space. Companies need financing, raw materials, employees, transportation, legal advice, etc. And none of it is free. Although resources are indispensable for production they must be carefully managed. The cold hard discipline of business dictates that companies must pay as little as possible so that they can produce their own items at a sellable price. The end result is that companies take and spend only what is necessary to run their businesses and resources that do get consumed are used to good effect. It is a process that ensures efficient and effective use of resources.

5. Recognition of Success and Failure

The recognition of success and failure in business is an almost exact parallel to what we see in nature. The successful survive and the failures die out. When companies fail, economists have called the process "creative destruction" because the disappearance of one company creates opportunities for others who step in and provide a better service. Although uncomfortable for those associated with failing companies, it is actually evidence of a healthy economic environment. One of the almost magical things about the free market is the unseen and unerringly accurate way it recognizes when a company is failing to provide its customers with what they currently need. The reasons a company might lose its customers are many and varied. It could be that: their product has become outdated, they have failed to control costs, the sales effort is inadequate, etc.

Whatever the cause, the market has a built-in capacity to repair itself and ensure that the customer gets what he needs.

6. Inheritance of Success

When a company is successful over an extended period of time it is generally good for reasons, and so long as the company continues to perform well the behaviors that drive results become a part of the culture and will be passed on to succeeding generations of employees. It can seem like a selfish and perhaps greedy process, but having expertise and a winning culture in-house and then passing it on to subsequent generations ultimately results in other companies having to up their game to compete. Although driven by self-interest the inheritance of winning strategies and even trade secrets by companies is actually beneficial to society as a whole.

7. Dependency on Others

In a properly functioning free market, companies do not control, they compete in a sustainable manner. Just like living creatures in a natural ecosystem, a company has to use externally produced items and provide sustenance to others. In other words, they have to become responsible citizens. Those who rapaciously eat up all competitors or exercise their power unfairly will eventually drift into becoming out of touch and hopelessly inefficient, and/or pay the price of government intervention.

8. Repeated Cycles

In the business world there have been many examples of one-hit wonders. Those enterprises sometimes look fantastic for a while, but quickly fade and fizzle out. Only by surviving multiple cycles can it be proven that a company is capable of being viable in the long run.

Although the timeframes are very different, the way companies come into existence and then disappear looks rather like the emergence of millions of lifeforms that have flourished and then

have ultimately died out. Which should not be too surprising—
they are playing to the same rules. Just like any plant or animal
species, companies are born, fulfill a purpose, and ultimately die
because they have been replaced by one that is younger, healthier,
or has attributes better suited to competing in the current
environment.

Evolution, Free Markets, and Humanity

There are, however, some big differences between evolution in
the natural and commercial worlds. The free market is an entirely
human construct—one of the many social mechanisms that have
been tried over the years and ultimately found to provide
benefits, such as religion and the rule of law. There are many
social mechanisms that have been retained and they all share one
essential commonality. Each and every one must accommodate
basic built-in human instinctual behaviors and also be subject to
modification based on the application of logic.

The free market pulls in and then uses quite a number of human
traits and it does so very effectively. Even aspects of human
nature that are often considered to be negative can actually have a
positive effect. The desire to regard one's own welfare above
others, sometimes seen as selfishness, encourages many to gain
more education, work harder, or invent useful items, etc., so it
benefits the individual while also benefitting society as a whole.

The desire to purchase an item can be entirely logical based on
the desire for utility, but it can also be affected by emotion. A
farmer wanting a plow, for example, will be primarily driven by a
desire to get one that works. On the other hand, someone
looking for an attractive vase to hold flowers will probably not
want an old Mason jar, even though it would likely perform the
basic function very well. Like it or not, we humans are a
confusing mix of emotional and practical needs and the two
often get mixed together when it comes time to make a purchase.

Archeological findings all over the globe reveal a basic need of
humans to acquire objects. It seems that people like to simply

own things for various reasons such as usefulness, aesthetics, and the desire to enhance their social status. The whole process is a wonderful mix of emotion and logic in which sellers try to figure out what will enhance peoples' lives and then make the product as attractive as possible through bright lights, colors, and all manner of other attractants. Once the buyer is sufficiently motivated the deal only goes down when a mutually agreed price is settled. And this results in one of the most honest relationships we are ever likely to experience. More than love, religion, and certainly more than politics. The seller wants the highest price as possible and the buyer wants the lowest. Regardless of whatever specific buying motives an individual might have, he will only part with cash once the object in question is seen to represent sufficient value. By the same token, the seller will not let the item go if the revenue is insufficient. That is not to say the deal makes everyone super happy, but so long as it happens without deception or coercion it is free, fair, and honest.

It does not always look like it, but our free market economy creates a society in which there are huge numbers of people actively searching for ways to improve other's existence by simply selling them something. People who have spent any time in a communist country understand how different our life is with all its bright colors and people actively wanting to please. A big contrast with the gray, badly lit stores with miserable salespeople who are just there to provide what is thought to be necessary. It is, therefore, small wonder that commerce operated through free markets has become such an important part of our everyday lives. It fulfills our purely emotional needs by providing art, music, and literature, as well as purely practical items like toilet cleaners, computers, and railways. But the majority of items we see are a combination of utility, beauty, and well-being, such as: architecturally significant buildings, expensive automobiles, and Apple iPhones. But commerce isn't just getting the products we want. The actual process appeals to our innate sense of fair play and equity because it maintains an environment in which those who strive to satisfy the needs of others are rewarded, and items offered for sale are seen to be priced fairly because they are open to competition.

Business Logic

Although the free market satisfies many of our practical and innate emotional needs, it would not work without the attribute that separates us from the rest of the natural world—our capacity for logical thought. The majority of what it takes to be commercially successful, particularly in today's modern economy, is not just concerned with the selling of products—that is just the end of long and complicated journey. Before products even get to market, there is often a chain of activities that involves market research, design, prototyping, manufacturing, transportation, along with a host of other support functions like accounting, human resources, legal issues, property acquisition, etc. All of these activities, in addition to many others not listed, require a great deal of logical thought, organization, and discipline. In fact, although satisfying customers can involve emotions, the majority of the time spent running businesses is cold hard "left brain" work.

All successful businesses have a very clear understanding of who they are and what they do. They develop strategies to achieve their stated goals. To do so, every single aspect of running a business must be evaluated in terms of cost effectiveness, which requires all relevant data to be gathered, analyzed, and accommodated within the overall plan. Once the detailed plans have been put together, mechanisms are put in place to monitor progress to ensure the plans are being adhered to, and the overall strategy is being maintained. Sounds simple, but none of this is easy—it requires logic, discipline, and hard work.

Putting It All Together

Nothing that humans get involved with works perfectly, and free markets are no exception. As with any activity there is always a tendency for someone to drop the occasional wrench into the gears and there can be times when rewards for success and the pain of failure seem excessive. But by and large the whole system works incredibly well because it brings together the essential elements of what it is to be human by fulfilling emotional needs and the application of logic.

The free market system clearly has a practical side to satisfy peoples' almost limitless and varied needs. Beyond the basic practical benefits of its operation, it also appeals to deep-seated emotional needs like the desire to fairly exchange goods and services for mutual benefit. It's okay to feel emotionally good about something, but there would be no goods to exchange without the application of imagination, innovation, physical work, organization, and a great deal of logical thought.

The format and mode of operation of any free market system are in a state of constant flux in response to constantly shifting demands and circumstances—all in an exquisitely responsive and constantly improving manner because it operates according to the same driving principles of evolution that demand nothing less than success. But what sets this form of continuous improvement apart from evolution in nature is the application of human intelligence. Instead of waiting for a company to die and another one to randomly appear, humans have learned some very important lessons over the years. These lessons have effectively taught us to fast track the evolutionary process by analyzing data and then working towards goals by: planning, monitoring performance, and making corrections. We have effectively figured out a way to make a course correction before total failure. This would be analogous to modifying the genetic message of a plant or animal during its lifetime so that it can survive   which simply does not happen.

Companies do not have to wait until the quarterly results come out to see if what they are doing is working. For example, daily, weekly, and monthly order reports can give a good indication of market changes and/or whether customers' needs are being met. Successful companies typically react immediately to analyze what is happening by talking to customers to find out if their tastes have changed, they are happy with the service, there is increased competition, etc. Once problems have been analyzed, remediation measures aimed at bettering the experience for the customer can be taken, which is one of the key drivers in continuous improvement.

Timely human intervention in business can, therefore, supercharge the evolution of companies and even entire industries because when they become aware of changing circumstances like competition, market disruptions, shortages of materials and labor, etc., they can make the necessary changes to remain viable. Death only comes to those companies who ignore the warning signs or cease to have the energy or wherewithal to compete.

The free market is clearly an effective and efficient mechanism when it comes to providing goods and services to society. But can the same principles be applied to government?

Chapter 10

Evolving Government

"I am not an advocate for frequent changes in laws and Constitutions. But laws and institutions must go hand in hand with the progress of the human mind. As that becomes more developed, more enlightened, as new discoveries are made, new truths discovered and manners and opinions change, with the change of circumstances, institutions must advance also to keep pace with the times. We might as well require a man to wear still the coat which fitted him when a boy as civilized society to remain ever under the regimen of their barbarous ancestors."

— Thomas Jefferson

Thomas Jefferson was right when he said our government should continually change to meet the demands produced by the ceaseless environmental and societal changes that define our human existence. Unfortunately, it would appear that our current politicians have either not heard such message or feel powerless to do anything in the way of radical changes. We cannot simply hope for our political system to heal itself and stand idly by as our living standards slide.

We will likely always have disagreements regarding national priorities, but improving the competency of government should not be a right versus left issue. The least well-off suffer most when the government performs poorly, but we all pay. The costs of the goods and services the government provides and/or controls ultimately have to be supported by private wealth-producers. If the government performs too much, too little, fails to regulate appropriately, or operates inefficiently companies will be less profitable, be unable to compete internationally, and their employees will suffer from layoffs or lagging wages. On the other hand, if the government encourages wealth creation, is responsive to the real needs of society, and performs efficiently, the country's economy will prosper and its companies made more competitive and able to support better paid workers. Why is that so important? Because only by having profitable companies <u>and</u> well-paid workers will we be able to support and protect our nation's living standards in an unpredictable world. Like it or not, we live in a global marketplace in which we either compete or get left behind by the rest of the world. So how do we get the government to step up and respond to the realities of the 21st Century and beyond?

If we accept that compliance with the rules of evolution brings about continuous and sustainable success in all competitive environments, like nature and free market commerce it would seem logical that the same principle should apply to nations. In America, we are lucky—we have a hard-working and adaptable population and strong innovative companies that will succeed if we let them. On the other hand, we have a government that consistently fails to recognize the real needs of the country and thereby adds to our overall operating costs and renders us less efficient as a nation. Government needs to be fixed. But how on earth do we apply the essential aspects of evolution to a process that thrives on truth bending at the political level, and tolerates inefficient program management when it comes to execution?

Business Model

Can we establish our real needs using appropriate data and then satisfy those needs by running the government as though it were a business operating in a competitive market place? The approach should work, because as described previously, the commerce-based free market has all of the essential elements of natural evolution. It also benefits from being able to employ human intellect and ingenuity, so it can quickly adapt to changing environments in terms of: resources, desires, needs, and capabilities. Continuous improvement is the inevitable result. The free market is able to operate successfully because it accommodates and is driven by innate human emotions, but then truth and logic step in and act as an overall unrelenting taskmaster. Although many sales in the commercial world are made on the basis of appealing to emotions, companies do not last long if the product does not function as promised or meet other needs of the customer. Reality always sets in. In politics things are quite different—the real needs of society are often not properly recognized, goals are seldom defined, detailed plans are not made, and to make it worse, progress is generally left un-monitored. Businesses are not run that way. Small wonder we like our favorite companies but get so disappointed with government.

Running the government like a business does not necessarily equate to having its various functions turn a profit and/or be operated by privatized companies. Government agencies turning a profit seldom makes sense because if it happens, they are likely doing so because they are either in a privileged monopolistic position or are able to hide some of their costs. Privatization can work very well in many circumstances because the very act of putting goods and services out for bid does a number of positive things. Firstly, it uncovers what might have been wasteful and unrecognized subsidies that were a misuse of resources. Secondly, it requires the agency to define what is required as an outcome—the desired result. Thirdly, it can foster competition which drives innovation and cost reductions. And fourthly, the agency is required to monitor progress relative to the stated commitments. Privatization is, therefore, a powerful option when it comes to having a government operate like a business. But it would be a mistake to think that one particular strategy is applicable in all circumstances. We would be better off concentrating on the overall goal, which is to have the government pursue the real needs of its customers and then provide value in the same way a business would.

Running the government like a business does not mean being blindly "pro-business" in the sense that we ask businesses what they want and then simply give it to them. All businesses want bigger revenues and lower costs, which makes sense because their primary responsibility is to their investors, and they can't be criticized for that—after all, that is what makes the whole capitalist thing work. But the government's primary responsibility is to the public—who act as both their investors and customers. Accordingly, the government must ensure that there is open and fair competition in all areas of the economy so that the public can be reasonably assured of getting value. Because companies' prime motivation is profit their priorities are different—they always want less competition. And there are some signs that they are getting what they want. The incestuous relationship between CEOs and board members who bid up each others' remuneration, the steady drift towards small, innovative companies being bought out, more consolidation, and increased profits without commensurate productivity, all taken together are a good indicator that employees and the public are not getting optimal value.

Accordingly, the government must foster an environment in which businesses can compete and prosper—not to just give them what they ask for. This is not the same as putting money in their pockets via subsidies, tax forgiveness, and mindless or lobbyist induced reductions in regulations. Instead, companies need the basics, like; access to capital; predictable legislation; low-priced utilities; good infrastructure; an educated, motivated workforce; and access to healthy markets, etc. All directed towards the holy grail of increased productivity, which is the only path to increased wealth and quality of life. As stated earlier, there are many instances in which the government should not interfere, there are times when the government can be a productive partner. For example, government investment in basic research has a proven track record of being the genesis of American leadership in new technologies that drive innovation and increase productivity. However, in an effort to cut government expenditures it would appear that we are now actively trying to pass the innovation lead onto China, because they are making bigger long-range investments in research that will likely be the primary drivers of the international economy in the future. We cannot let them overtake us.

Running the government like a business means using business disciplines and logic to recognize and set national priorities, allocate resources, and manage progress to ensure goals are achieved in an efficient and effective manner within the confines of democracy—for the benefit of the public. If the business logic approach is adopted, political candidates will not be judged on their left or right credentials, but on the quality of their ideas, the solidity of their plans, and ultimately on their ability to deliver promised results. For progress to be made, partisan ideologies that dictate <u>how</u> problems should be addressed must be set aside and replaced with a business-like focus on clearly defined objectives based on properly understood definitions of what is needed, followed up with and an unwavering commitment to efficiently achieve the required results, whether or not the means and methods comply with ideology or not. Who cares how it gets done so long as we get value and it works?

The first step is to decide what the overarching national goal, or a vision that guides the formation of detailed plans necessary to ensure long-term success. A possible vision is:

> *To enhance the performance of our democracy, thereby ensuring that America remains the most powerful nation on Earth, with equal opportunity and living standards that are at least equal to those of other wealthy nations.*

This means that America will be preeminent in terms of military and financial strength, and the vision will not be achieved at the expense of the middle class, the poor, or the democratic process. In fact, the vision requires that we should strive to be "best in class" in all respects. It also demands a more sophisticated approach than just cutting taxes and regulations. Those policies could very well spur the economy and help companies become more profitable. But they do not address how to enhance our social structures by addressing urgent issues like wealth and income inequality, the worker-less economy, affordable health care, equal opportunity, efficient infrastructure of all kinds, and getting an adequately educated workforce, etc., etc. And mindless automatic payments to redress the symptoms of societal dysfunction intended to protect the middle class and poor will not work either. Continued unaffordable payments that are inefficient and/or ineffective will eventually bring about the collapse of programs because wealth generation provided by the private sector is the prime provider of all aspects of social well-being, and it can only support so much. In short, government expenditures and regulations must be carefully aimed, sufficient, confined to what is necessary, and managed in an effective and efficient manner.

Business Approach

Getting the government to start thinking and performing like a business seems like a tall order, and it is. Fortunately, it would appear that the country has recognized that our political system is not up to the current task and is ripe for some big changes. The election of Donald Trump was a clear indication that voters wanted something completely different, and they weren't afraid to upset the apple cart to get it. The old partisan divide was looking old and tired. Apart from his populist rhetoric Trump's big appeal for many was his proven ability in business. Surely this powerful man could cut through the fog of partisan politics, work with both sides, and get things working. Unfortunately, that did not happen. After the election, it became evident that he was more adept at brand management than making deals with anyone other than those who had bought into his message.

It is true that Donald Trump possessed one of the necessary skills required for all businesses, the ability to create an image and sell it. But it turns out that he was not able to follow through and demonstrate many of the other competencies or character traits required of the leader of a large organization. Which would not have come as a total surprise if we had acted like a business and been able to get a truthful resumé at the time of hiring. For example, the image of the self-made billionaire has turned out to be more than a little inaccurate. Although completely different from anyone else who has ever occupied the White House, Donald Trump is similar to many other politicians we have seen over the years in one essential respect. He is strong on appealing to emotions and cultivating an image, but unable to identify the nation's real problems and weak on execution.

But let's not give up on the concept of bringing business expertise into government just because we tried it once and it did not work out well. It is true that there have been many disappointments when business leaders have tried their hand at politics, but there have also been a number of successes, or at least mixed bags. Whatever you think of Michael Bloomberg's politics, his tenure as mayor of New York showed just how successful a leader can be when sound business strategies are applied to the execution side of government. He called on experiences gained when he built his own highly successful business. Much of what he did in government to improve efficiency and quality of life of New Yorkers was based on the importation of private industry expertise. Much of it is now taken for granted by many working in modern companies, like being open to the ideas of others, setting realistic goals, applying a statistical results-based approach, monitoring progress, and giving managers the freedom to operate. Obviously, there were some successes and some failures, but overall his efforts made New York a better place to live and work.

Although the sales talents of Donald Trump and the management skills of Michael Bloomberg are important, they do not represent everything needed for a leader in a properly functioning democracy. Applying the essential elements of the free market to the democratic process requires some imaginative thinking.

Customer-Focused and Effective Government

If we are to fix our government it is essential that we highlight some of the similarities and differences between politics and every-day commerce and thereby explain how business disciplines can and should be applied to our democracy. The goal of government should be to efficiently and continuously tailor its services just as a large company that sells custom goods and services in a complex market can never stand still because it has to meet their customers' ever-changing needs. Can we adopt the essential disciplines of business and thereby transfer the same processes to the operation of our government? Let's hope so, because our government represents the biggest provider of goods and services in the country and one way or another we all pay.

Below is a description of the various steps involved in providing goods and services commercially, together with a description of how the essential disciplines can be incorporated into our democracy:

1. Product Development

Before complex items are offered for sale in a commercial market, they must be carefully designed so they can be delivered at an acceptable cost and represent value to the customer. In today's Western economies most effort is directed towards satisfying wants rather than needs. All of the effort put into convincing people to buy something better, newer, or shinier is really just a testament to how successful our modern societies have become. We are no longer fighting to survive—we now forage for whatever we think will make our lives more satisfying and comfortable. But the process does not get out of control because it is regulated by the free market which has built-in disciplines that control both production and consumption of all goods and services. Companies try hard to produce only what they can sell and people are restricted by their incomes and credit card limits.

Politicians tend to do much the same thing as motivated commercial sellers. Once the perceived basic needs have been satisfied, they move on to discovering what the electorate might like to have and then sell it to them. Since getting what you want is so pleasurable, the seemingly generous or just plain appealing politicians get re-elected and the cycle is repeated. At this point, the politics start to look quite different from the commercial model. The trouble is that the self-correcting disciplines of commercial transactions do not kick in for a number of reasons. The biggest one being that no one feels sufficient pain from: a failure to establish needs, poor products, overproduction, or overconsumption. Once the government starts to supply goods and services it seldom sees reason to stop because although they have a bad product, they do not get immediate feedback from the electorate who know little about the program in terms of effectiveness, efficiency of delivery, and cost. Secondly, the electorate does not feel the pain of overpaying for something that doesn't work or that they might not particularly want because the costs are covered by government borrowing or what feels like someone else's taxes. This is not intended to be a partisan jibe aimed purely at left-wing politicians who provide nice-sounding services without too much regard for having to raise taxes. Right-wing politicians who tend to offer tax breaks without the fortitude to cut popular services are no better. In fact, the effects of targeted tax cuts can be even more pernicious. They are generally pieces of social engineering intended to reward certain behaviors or favored classes. Not only do they complicate the tax code, they tend to stick because no one wants to be seen as the person who is taking something away—the unfunded giveaway typically just gets added to the deficit.

Since it is easier to pander to voters by satisfying their wants as opposed to their needs, politicians very often give lip service to, or totally ignore, what is actually required. Which is quite alarming. We urgently need to prepare for what is going to happen as we get further into the 21st century by doing everything necessary to make our nation more productive and internationally competitive such as getting the deficit under control; preparing for increased automation; recognizing and nurturing technologies and industries of the future; ensuring cybersecurity; mitigating global warming; making education effective and appropriate; building efficient infrastructure; making health care affordable; reforming the criminal justice system; overhauling our democracy; and ensuring the nation is not taken advantage of by companies that are not subject to genuine competition. It's quite a list.

In the commercial world, money is an extremely valuable resource, so it is not directed towards projects that do not offer a clear path to measurable success. Success has to be defined in terms of numbers, such as sales, revenue, resources, costs, and timetables. Proposed courses of action are typically presented in enough detail that they can be judged for viability prior to approval to proceed. Once given the green light, the original proposal can be used as the basis of a plan that can be monitored as implementation proceeds. It is suggested that we demand our politicians do something similar so they do not get away with offering pie-in-the-sky proposals designed to conform to party dogma and phony emotional appeals to fear, patriotism, or romanticism but lack rigorous analysis and supporting evidence.

The 2016 presidential election was replete with broad promises that had no foundation in reality. It is clear we have a perfect opportunity to judge some sloppy and ill-considered promises that were made in the run-up to the election. A proposal to reduce health care costs by opening insurance markets across state lines sounded good since many were not in favor of Obamacare—and lower insurance rates always sounds good. Dismantling Obamacare didn't happen because there was no serious plan to replace it. Reciting simple one-liners, like "repeal and replace," on something as important as health care should not be seen as acceptable for many reasons. One of the main being that it does not address the real problem which is the underlying cost of delivery. In contrast, Mexico paying for a wall did not require a detailed analysis since it was so obviously not going to happen. Additionally, throwing out unrealistic estimates of enough growth from tax reductions to pay down the deficit without any kind of substantiation must not be acceptable either. For example, simple questions like "when and where has that ever happened before?" and "where are the numbers to back up the calculations?" would need to be answered.

Without the built-in disciplines that come with commercial offerings it will be necessary to design some and insert them into what is offered at election time. It is unrealistic to imagine replicating the pain of buying more than you can afford and then maxing out your credit card or having our government go out of business because they institute a questionable program that goes badly. We could, however, install the same kind of disciplines that companies use to predict the likely success of a product or service and only then give the purchaser (taxpayer) the ability to evaluate whether or not the program will likely provide value as advertised.

Experience tells us that it is unrealistic to think that individual politicians will self-impose the discipline required to ensure their electioneering messages are sound and workable. It's simply harder to sell a good government plan than one that offers something "free" which has the added benefit of taking away pain—particularly yours. It is a lot less exciting and old habits simply die hard. Salespeople in the commercial world have discipline imposed from the corporate office—companies cannot tolerate incorrect claims of performance or unrealistic delivery promises. If they are to stay in business, they must protect their reputation for honesty and reliability. Right now, we do not hold our political parties to the standards we demand of the private companies we deal with. We let them get away with vague, unsupported promises and then forgive them because we are told they tried hard—then we elect them again. That has got to stop, but don't expect it any time soon unless we voters take their responsibilities as seriously as we do when we buy a new product from Amazon.

Such a lot of what makes private industry work is careful thought, commitment, and corporate and personal responsibility. Right now, our parties appear happy to see candidates make all sorts of overly optimistic predictions. So long as the candidate gets elected, they do not really care since the promises are forgotten. There is no real commitment from the candidate or the party because they are not suffering any consequences.

In order to emulate proposals made by companies in the private sector, we must demand that every proposition a candidate makes must specify goals, resources, costs, and timelines along with supporting documentation. In addition, the relevant party must analyze the proposal and confirm it is appropriate and achievable. The proposals and their party endorsement will be published on the internet so that it can be studied by any member of the public and any errors identified.

If we could set a standard for identifying real needs and providing credible plans to satisfy them, it is easy to imagine an environment in which politicians can no longer successfully present poorly thought out proposals designed to be consistent with what people want to hear. In this future world, they would be forced to exercise their responsibility by competing with properly conceived proposals with independent expert backup documentation that demonstrates results.

2. Sales

Before a salesperson approaches a potential buyer, they need to be sure they are talking to the right person. That sounds obvious, but sometimes a sales pitch that accurately describes value based on a combination of performance and price ends up being judged by a member of the purchasing department who has little technical knowledge and is often primarily interested in making a cost comparison. If the decision is made on the basis of initial cost, the manager responsible for implementation can be saddled with excessive labor costs or other inefficiencies. On the other hand, line managers have been known to be overly influenced by a great presentation and ignore or not seek out competing offers. To get the full picture, companies typically make clear specifications describing performance criteria and then compare costs or involve the end user who can recognize the real-life implications of cost and performance. Whether purchases are made by individuals or representatives of companies, the focus must always be on a clear understanding of value to the end user.

In our democracy, the end user is the electorate because it is they who must ultimately pay for what the politicians enact. Although it might seem like a simple relationship, ordinary voters are actually offered a product that has been pre-sold to other non-paying customers. They are the donors, lobbyists, and party members. Only after the platform has been vetted by those who have money and/or influence can the customer who pays the bill get a look in.

To make the political process more like the commercial world in which paying customers are actively pursued and made the central focus, the first step will be to remove the impediments to direct access, as noted in Chapter 7.

> Money has a profound effect on the operation of our government. The need for continual fundraising has a negative effect on politicians' effectiveness and use of time since it requires a presence and never ending requests for donations. Time would be better spent solving real issues. We have gotten so used to politicians pandering to their donors such as: lawyers, pharmaceutical companies, unions, defense contractors, etc. that we have become inured to the fact that this is a very corrupt process. Even our foreign policy gets to be affected. The spectacle of our politicians falling over themselves to become the most passionate supporters of Israel to get contributions from a pro-Israel casino owner should make us all think carefully about what drives important issues. But it all gets overlooked because it has become a normalized part of our system. Rightly or

wrongly, the Supreme Court has ruled that political donations are a form of free speech and therefore protected by the Constitution. The argument goes that a person has the right to donate money because it is the only way to get the message out. That might be so, but what if this results in a politician favoring the views of donors above those of the electorate?

One way or another we have to allow free speech without letting certain peoples' voices have more power than others just because they have money. How about donations going to a single pot that then gets distributed equally? If your real goal is to get your message out as opposed to buying influence why would you care that an equal amount goes to the other side? If there is to be a competition of ideas, getting the other side to speak would just enhance the discussion.

Lobbyists clearly affect what gets served up to us, but we generally don't see the process—it all happens behind the scenes. The medical industry has done a fantastic job of protecting its interests over the years, so we don't seem to hear anything serious about reigning in health care costs. Trial lawyers have had a cozy relationship established with the Democratic Party for a long time, so there is little doubt as to why they oppose tort reform. The Republican Party is in the thrall of the NRA to the extent that they can more or less dictate who gets nominated as a Republican candidate for the House or Senate. If recent polling is to be believed, this results in moderate gun control propositions like background checks going nowhere even though more than 90% of the population support them.

Reigning in lobbyists is a hugely difficult task because they have become part of the system. Just to make this issue more complicated, some lobbying often has beneficial effects. Lawmakers writing bills should be informed of potential downsides before the laws are written. What sounds like a good idea to a politician might actually have a negative effect on certain communities or industries, for example. The solution might just be openness—possibly instituting a rule that says when lobbyists meet with members of Congress, they must be in open sessions with the public invited. At least we would have the opportunity to see and hear what is going on.

<u>Safe Gerrymandered Districts</u> have a corrosive effect on our political system because they encourage extreme views and the punishment of anything that looks like accommodation. Party members, otherwise known as "hardliners", or more kindly "the party faithful", naturally set the agenda and establish the platform for their party. There is nothing wrong with that because they are the people who care enough about how the country should be run that they actually put effort into doing something. But the process can go awry in safe districts—because the results are so one-sidedly red or blue that the outcome of the election is more or less pre-ordained. In these cases the candidates tend to represent a somewhat extreme version of what the party stands for on certain issues. Moderate members of the same party might be a bit unhappy with some of these positions, but they go along because the candidate is, after all, our guy and therefore much better than the opposition. It follows that even though these extremely partisan positions are supported by a minority of the population, they become the mainstream position of the established parties as a whole. Uncompetitive races sometimes come into being because they are simply a reflection of the views of people living in particular areas and locations. But sometimes they are the result of gerrymandering, which is a process by which the size and shape of the electoral map is artificially altered to favor one particular party. The problem is that there is currently no great hurry to change things because

both established parties have their own safe seats, and that makes for a more comfortable situation for both sides. They simply don't have to work hard to keep their seats. Having gerrymandered safe seats is clearly an affront to democracy because the will of the majority is set aside by a system that favors certain voters above others. Not only that, it increases partisanship because candidates can recycle outdated and extreme dogma and ignore new ideas.

All electoral districts should be redrawn to ensure everyone's vote is equal and elections are made competitive, which is clearly possible because there are many successful state models that have already been applied. No state should be allowed to maintain districts that have been engineered to favor either political party. Instead, each state should be required to organize and demonstrate it has a competitive and fair system.

The intended goal is to have politics look more like the sale of goods and services in a competitive free market environment. If voters are given the same respect as paying customers in the commercial world, they will be offered a clearly defined proposal that has been crafted for them, not for third parties with a vested interest in the outcome of the election. And when the sale is made, it will be on the basis of a one vote per person, not one in which some of the electorates' votes have been purposely devalued.

3. Delivery

It would be logical to think that spending your own money should always be a painful process and avoided if at all possible. But, for the most part, it doesn't seem to be that way. When we make a purchase, we give little thought to the fact that everything we see and hear is part of a manufactured environment that has been carefully crafted to relieve us of our hard earned cash and actually feel so good about the experience that we willingly return and do it again. It all seems so natural and pleasant that it is easy to forget that the whole business of satisfying customers is an incredibly complex process that is driven by cold hard logic and discipline. Identifying the constantly changing perceived needs and wants of customers is not always easy, but that is only the first step. Competition then dictates that the required goods and services are provided at the lowest cost possible. It becomes a delicate balancing act. Making customers feel that they are the center of the universe must be tempered by minimizing costs and getting optimum value out of product development, transportation, warehousing, staff, real estate, sales and service, marketing, utilities, etc., etc. Behind the scenes it's a dog-eat-dog world in which only the fittest survive. There is no room for wooly thinking or indiscipline at any stage of the delivery process. Once approved and given the go ahead to proceed, every major project in the private sector is required to have a detailed plan for implementation which includes a defined goal, resources, budget, and schedule. Vague pronouncements like "We will greatly improve......, and costs will be slashed......," just don't cut it. As the work proceeds, progress is monitored at regular intervals to ensure the project remains on track.

It's just not like that in the world of government since politicians are elected on the basis of promises that often go unfulfilled and failure seldom gets punished. Consequently, our government does not experience the same kind of imperative to deliver in a consistently competent and efficient manner. And we have just gotten used to it. We are expected to be satisfied with snappy sound bite promises followed up with little or no progress reporting as reality unfolds post-election. What is the plan? Is it working? How much is it costing? Who knows?

Right now, the electorate does not have a good way to monitor progress of programs in terms of cost, goal achievement, or schedule. Whether or not promised goals are being met is virtually unknowable to the average person and therefore no one is held to account. The cycle of promises being made, forgotten, and then new ones made in time for the next election just continues.

It is clear that we need to facilitate the implementation of a system based on rigorous goal setting, planning, and subsequent monitoring of all programs which will emulate the management practices of successful companies.

If this were to happen, and the time comes to actually implement programs, a more detailed plan should be produced and presented in a standard format on the internet which will allow the public to monitor and make comment. The following will be provided:

a) A clear statement that defines goals, cost implications, implementation schedules
b) A plan that defines resources and key dates for attainment of final and essential interim goals
c) Endorsement from the relevant parties and qualified experts that confirm the proposal is realistic and attainable
d) A description of how success will be measured during and after implementation
e) A statement of responsibility—either personally or with other named members of Congress who commit to making appropriate laws and ensuring efficient delivery

Progress reporting will follow a standard format such that movement toward goal achievement can be monitored at preset intervals. One scenario would be to have relatively simple monthly reports that give percentage completion of action line items together with corresponding expenditures so that cost at completion or long-term operational costs can be accurately predicted. Quarterly reports will be more detailed and include an executive summary that describes any significant events together with actions to be taken to get results back on track, remedy schedule slippage and/or cost issues. In addition, detailed breakdowns of subcategories of work together with supporting documentation will be available for inspection when necessary. The electorate will, therefore, be able to see if the promises made in the original proposal are being achieved. It could be argued that the foregoing would subject the government to a great deal of extra work. Experience would suggest otherwise, particularly now, because modern technology is capable of collecting all relevant data and processing it into usable information in real time. Once the progress report has been set up, the process of reporting percentage completion of line items, outcomes, and relevant costs is not onerous. It works in private industry. Why would it not work for the government?

4. Best Practices
Companies by and large do not like competition because it is hard to stay one step ahead of others who want to take their customers, but there is no alternative if they are to survive. Competition acts as the most demanding professor at the University of Hard Knocks who eventually manages to teach his students how to operate their businesses using best practices.

It would be easy to imagine that our most successful new companies have stumbled onto new ideas and technologies and have thereby been able to ride the wave to wealth and happiness. It is true that moving into the hi-tech universe in the recent past has held certain obvious advantages over old industries, like coal and asbestos mining, but being in the right industrial sector has never been a guarantee of success. It's great to have a good idea and be in the right business, but that alone does not bring about long-term survival. Even in the golden age of American automobile manufacturing there were winners and losers. The truth is that the unforgiving rules of business apply no matter what, whenever or wherever goods and services are sold. Customers have to be presented with something that represents better value than what is offered by competitors time and time again. Businesses have to be continuously innovative, predicting what customers will want, repeatedly adjusting when they make mistakes, and then delivering in the most cost-effective manner. It is a brutal system, but it keeps companies lean and responsive and it has always been clear that some have been better than others. One pattern seems to emerge—those that have been successful have done so by sticking to the basics which include being continually focused on their core capabilities and making the adjustments necessary to meet the demands of an ever-changing marketplace. On the other hand, those that have refused to adapt or been unable to change have either fallen by the wayside or have descended into mediocrity, surviving in an almost zombie-like state.

Over time, human progress has made huge leaps forward as new technologies are introduced: steel, steam, electricity, railroads, telephones, transistors, internet, microchips, GPS, etc. These technologies have all bestowed tremendous benefits, but none of it would have been possible without companies making the technologies practical and economical enough to use in everyday life. The power of steam did not transport anyone until a boiler and all the machinery to make tractive power and railway lines were designed, manufactured, and sold by well-run companies. Having the idea is good and necessary, but it only becomes useful when people come together and manage the entire process. In our modern capitalist free market system that means having multiple companies competing to translate good ideas into useful products at affordable prices. And those companies can only do so sustainably if they establish and maintain sound management practices to control the basics of running a business.

So, what are the successful business basics? It seems like everyone has an opinion. There has been a long list of "business gurus" over the years, all with their own particular theories regarding what is necessary to run companies successfully. Logic would suggest that they cannot all be correct, but maybe that isn't the point. Their opinions might have varied somewhat, but they always put heavy emphasis on the necessity of good management. Perhaps the process of just making people re-evaluate what they are doing has had positive effects. In any event, the scientific approach to management seems to have helped. It is unlikely to be a coincidence that the majority of influential gurus have been American and that our companies have always been at the cutting edge of management techniques. Over the years, America has developed management expertise that is second to none because it focuses on the basics. Recently, a group of economists studied the performance of more than 10,000 organizations in 20 countries, focusing on three commonly accepted management techniques: setting targets, rewarding performance, and measuring results. They discovered that America has the best-managed companies. Superior management accounts for about a quarter of the 30% productivity gap between America and Europe. The economists also suggest the main driver of this superiority is competition, because it forces constantly improving performance. American business shows every sign that it can continue to adapt and compete successfully. It is capable of making innovations and then acquiring adequate financing to get things going. Just compare the formation of new big businesses between 1975 and 2007: there were 52 in America versus 12 in Europe. Moreover, the trend right now seems to be giving America an even bigger edge because the newest big companies are typically based on life-changing disruptive products and concepts. Who could possibly imagine life without the likes of Microsoft, Intel, Google, Facebook, and Apple? This largely explains why businesses this side of the Atlantic are consistently more profitable than those headquartered in Europe.

If we are to progress as a nation, we must do the same as companies: adopt best practice management strategies that work in American business and apply them to government operations.

In the broadest sense, we know very well what works day in and day out in the real world. Establish motivated and competent teams and then keep them focused on the basics. There are essentially six steps to getting something done:

1. *Define Objectives*
   Otherwise known as "what you want" as a desired outcome, which must be defined by numbers and bound by time. Even in a business environment this can be a very difficult thing to get right. Since the exercise is so difficult, even companies make complicated statements of objectives that really boil

down to saying, "we will try harder and get better at what we do.......with less". Very admirable, but it is pie-in-the-sky thinking that is similar to what we currently do in politics. But this is clearly not consistent with best practices. Successful companies treat the issue of setting objectives seriously, and it becomes the impetus for innovation which drives the entire company to higher levels of performance.

The concept of defining objectives as a first step rather than just employing tactics and tools that have been used before can be applied to any human endeavor that requires concerted and coordinated action. We spend too much time on arguments that assume things have to be done the way they always have. General Patton, one of the most effective generals in WWII, certainly understood the value of establishing the goals of a mission rather than imposing a way of doing things: *"Never tell people how to do things. Tell them what to do, and they will surprise you with their ingenuity"*. *War As I Knew It* (1947), by George S. Patton

Is our political system capable of defining objectives? You bet it is. John F. Kennedy's proclamation that America would land men on the moon by the end of the 1960s was a clear statement of an objective that was bold, achievable, and limited by time. The president had no idea how the goal would be achieved, but it galvanized the nation and set in place a program that benefited industry, science, education, and the morale of the nation. Our country has not yet gained the status of what might be called perfection, so there are a number of possible avenues for improvement. The first step is to recognize that choosing objectives is vitally important because they will define our success in the foreseeable future.

2. *Plan the Work*
   Once an objective has been defined the next step is to plan how it can be achieved. The very best objectives create a mindset that instills urgency and motivation. Rather than look at problems and think about how existing teams, equipment,

and other resources can be tweaked to improve effectiveness, a bold objective often requires an approach based on first principles. For example, an objective concerning the criminal justice system should be based on desired outcomes like having felons becoming properly functioning citizens, rather than having more or less people locked up. As in the world of commerce, all plans should be formulated in such a way that progress towards ultimate success can be monitored in terms of results, resources, costs, and timetables.

3. *Execute the plan*
    Execution is where thoughts and ideas meet reality. There is a commonly held belief among those of a right-wing persuasion that the government cannot do anything efficiently. Although that is clearly not the case in all instances, it is true that private industry generally gets things done faster and more efficiently. But it is often an unfair comparison. Those in private commerce have a head start, they generally have the freedom to operate as opposed to those in the government who work in a system designed to ensure there is no room for corruption. The lucky managers in private industry are typically judged only by results—who cares if you cut corners and spend too much on pencils, so long as you were successful? It really comes back to the necessity for competition to improve all aspects of delivery including competition. So how do we apply the essence of competition to government? We must first recognize that even in business competition does not necessarily involve the acquisition and payment of money. Successful sales people often tell you that they appreciate getting a bonus for meeting targets, but cash is only part of the reward. Equally important is competing and being recognized for what they have done. The sales figures are in fact a measure of their success and how they compare to their peers. Similarly, good and fair competition can also be made part of the lives of government employees too. Most governmental departments are not staffed by people who are unhappy to be there and just fill in time until the end of the day and eventually retire.

But that can happen if they are allowed or pushed into serving out their sentences in a thankless, unappreciative atmosphere that places compliance above achievement. Creating competition in terms of execution can and should be introduced into all levels of government, but it will require adopting the essential steps of defining objectives, planning, and a rigorous analysis of success that requires comparison with peers in other locations. Or simply being challenged to demonstrate value and then have success published.

Although it is getting into the weeds of local government, the issue of garbage collection can provide a simple example where similar government agencies can see themselves as competitors. Clearly, every municipality wants to keep their costs as low as possible and they very often approach the issue with their own political bias. Conservative administrations typically move to privatize all operations, while those with a liberal leaning sometimes assume that their own forces will be more efficient and pleasing to their voter base. The "privatize everything" movement sometimes requires individuals to deal directly with any competent company they see fit, which satisfies the competition requirement—but is it good for the home owner? Probably not. The reason being that although you get your garbage picked up by your lowest bidder, there will likely be three of four separate collection trucks passing your house every week which is highly inefficient and obviously someone has to pay. But surely that is better than having the work done by direct hires who don't have to compete with anyone and are difficult to discipline or fire. And who knows if the operation is being run efficiently or not? A more cost efficient and transparent approach could be for the municipality to contract out the work of collection to companies for a defined period. This would avoid the duplication of multiple companies traveling the same route and also avoid the opaque and competition-free, self-performing strategy. Which one should be chosen? The answer is actually relatively simple—the one that satisfies the requirement of meeting the demands of the objective which is the lowest cost and most reliable service. Once a municipality has defined the criteria for success (perhaps cost per household per mile per week) they can judge themselves against other municipalities in similar circumstances— providing the performance data is published and available to everyone. The first benefit will be that they can actually become aware of their own performance and then start to research how to improve or give the message to their citizens that they are not paying too much. Maybe a reason to be re-elected?

Garbage collection is not the most important issue we have to face—it is provided only as an example of how governments can move towards a situation in which their performance can be measured and then used to improve execution. On a national scale, issues tend to be somewhat bigger and more complex, but the same basic principles apply. Fortunately, there is plenty of information out there to compare one city or state's performance relative to another and even make international comparisons. Could it be that Europeans are providing certain services in a more cost-effective manner? Perhaps we can learn from them and become more efficient? If we adopt the "best-in-class" approach that is common in many industries, we will be able to identify targets for improvement and then adjust our programs to ensure we compete successfully.

4. *Check*

Once execution is underway, it is essential to take stock at regular intervals to answer the all-important questions:

a) Are we working to the plan? Once the work starts it is common to have people lose focus and start doing things their own way. This happens for a myriad of reasons, like the team has found a better way of doing things. Mostly, the reasons are not so good, and people have become undisciplined or gone back to the way they used to do things.

b) We might find that we are working to the plan, but are we still on track to meet the ultimate objective? There is a saying in military circles that a plan only lasts as long as it takes for the first shot to be fired. And that is more or less the case in the business world. Although there are likely no bullets flying, the real world has a habit of getting in the way of what looked good on paper. The trouble is that many people start to think that since the plan was written down and agreed to, it represents a collection of rules that must be followed—it has, in effect become the objective. The consequences of which can be stultifying, and lead to unfortunate aspects of a rigid bureaucracy. It can happen in private industry, but the effect is much more common in governmental operations. There must be mechanisms to intercept and deal with plans that are not working—there is no shame in changing things to get back on track.

5. *Make Revisions*
Things go sideways—that's the nature of the world generally and human activities in particular. On the odd occasion, the checking process reveals that everything is fine and the objective will be reached with no problem at all. In the majority of circumstances, however, issues will be discovered. If people are not keeping to the established plan, immediate remedial action is required, and this generally involves some sort of reinforcement of what constitutes individual and team responsibilities. If everyone is keeping to the plan and there is still a drift away from the path, it is necessary to get the operation refocused onto the real mission of meeting the objective, which might require a reallocation of resources. In any event, a remedial plan must be put in place and this now becomes the basis of action in the future.

The requirement for keeping things on track by continually refocusing on the end goal of the mission is generally understood in the commercial world, but it is not quite so easy in politically driven government operations largely because the Objective, Plan, Execute, Check, and Revise principles are not generally applied. And if they are, the electorate does not normally get to see what is going on. Which doesn't make sense. They should be able to see if promises have been kept and whether or not they are getting what they paid for.

6. Leadership
It almost goes without saying that successful businesses require good leaders. There are a number of different styles of leadership, but it appears that no company can survive without a competent person at the helm. It is true that there are many examples of modern companies being led by individuals who are tech savvy and also driven to succeed, but those who are still around are usually also adept at being successful leaders and not just ambitious tech geeks. As well as being the person responsible for the big decisions, leaders of companies are really there to establish a culture that facilitates sustainable success. "People have an irritating habit of doing what you tell them to do" is an intentionally provocative statement intended to get peoples' attention and start them thinking about how to successfully manage people. It sounds like a stupid thing to say—surely the problem is that people do not do what they're supposed to and that is why things are a mess? Well, true, but the rationale for the statement centers around what telling people to do really means.

What it does not mean is: the email you sent out, what got put on the notice board, what you stood up and said at the last meeting, or even what it says in the company HR manual, etc. What it does mean is your actions and reactions that you exhibit on a daily basis. It is the way you demand discipline in achieving goals, require respect for all members of staff, encourage innovation and risk taking, etc. In other words, it is the culture that has been established, which usually involves "leading by example," that drives the behaviors of the employees in a company. For good or ill, people adopt the culture they see around them and believe that this is what they have really been "told to do."

Things are not too different in the world of politics. It was not the farmers and tradespeople of America that drafted the Declaration of Independence and wrote the Constitution. They were too busy earning a living and raising their families to be concerned with elevated discussions about basic human freedoms and the ins and outs of creating a durable democracy. And who can blame them? If you are responsible for putting food on the table and providing shelter for your family, you have more immediate issues calling on your time and energy. But that is not to say that everyday people cannot be roused to action if they are convinced that there are important issues that go beyond mundane daily responsibilities. Indeed, we humans are hard-wired to actively search out and follow leaders who are strong, and capable of bringing us together for communal action.

Although we think of democracy as an instrument designed to reflect the will of the people, reality is a little more complex. The Founding Fathers knew very well that blindly going along with the majority would lead to all sorts of problems including a form of mob rule in which minority views and interests could be suppressed and harassed. By many measures, the Founding Fathers represent leadership at its best. They recognized a need for a well-designed democratic structure and then they set about putting it in place with the agreement (or perhaps acquiescence) of the general public. They established a mechanism and a culture based on freedom, justice, and democracy that has stood the test time. At no point in our history has the value of leadership been so evident and so successful.

Leadership in democracies is not a one-off thing that happened years ago and is no longer needed because the system is so good we can put it on autopilot. The majority of people are still primarily concerned with the day-to-day concerns of earning a living and doing the best for their families. They do not want to be consumed by the running of government. All they want is political leaders who will offer them reasonable solutions and then ensure the government fulfills its obligations. It is not the average citizen's job to formulate foreign policy or maintain fiscal discipline, etc. The fact is that our country has always needed good political leaders who have been able to understand the nation's wants, needs, and aspirations and then garner enough support to convert dreams into reality. The job requirements include: conviction, courage, vision, showmanship, and basic management skills. But it also requires an understanding of the value of taking the long view and aspiring to higher values, rather than just chasing short-term fixes to problems that offer immediate popular gratification. Too often we end up with politicians possessing little more than ego and showmanship.

It is clear that none of the operational improvements described above will ever see the light of day without the right leaders coming forward and taking the necessary action. The sad truth is that the electorate's only real choice is between what our various leaders actually have to offer. And right now, that's a seriously depressing thought, particularly when you think about the choices available in the 2016 Presidential election. Two candidates with different demonstrably evident ethical challenges. But both were supported by those fully prepared to forgive and even endorse their behaviors. The power of committed support to a leader was clearly demonstrated when it was revealed that despite Russian hacking in the election and various other nefarious acts 40% of Republicans had joined with Trump and now considered Russia an ally or friend. The Republican Party had changed from denigrating Democrats for weakness on Russia to being the one with more grassroots support for a cozier relationship—primarily because of the new leader's exhortations.

In the present political environment, it is unlikely that many of our existing politicians will step up to the plate because honesty and long term-solutions are simply not rewarded. How can politicians proposing cold-shower realism possibly compete with those that offer something free and play to our tribal fears? Unfortunately, we have something of a chicken and egg situation —it is hard to imagine today's politicians fixing a system that is currently keeping them in a job.

Non-Partisan Future
Well, not necessarily completely non-partisan, but even being less so would get us closer to having a responsive democracy that serves our needs more effectively. The political climate right now smothers individual needs by insisting that all members think and behave in a prescribed manner with accommodation seen as weakness that lets the side down. But that does not reflect how most of us think. For many people motivating issues like climate change, abortion, gun rights, fiscal responsibility, and health care are totally unrelated. But currently, you can't separate them when it comes time to vote.

The goal of this chapter is to describe ways in which we can apply the lessons of life and business to the world of politics and thereby bring clarity and honesty to government. Most of what we have right now is a choice between promises of happiness without raising taxes, and a more comfortable future that will probably cost more—neither of which have worked particularly well up to now. The removal of corrupting influences like money, lobbying, and gerrymandering will be a huge step forward. And once people have been offered the opportunity to compare political solutions that have data-supported realistic goals together with plans for implementation, the focus will almost certainly shift away from unthinking party affiliated voting and move towards data-driven solutions. When our politicians start to see which way the wind is blowing, they will likely cross the aisle and support proposals that manifestly satisfy a need. For example, who would not support a solid proposal to cut our health care costs and improve outcomes, particularly when the plan comes with a transparent method of measuring success during and after implementation?

If the suggested changes are implemented a new mindset will inevitably develop, and then foster open and fair competition between solutions rather the battle of ideologies that we currently endure. This new environment will recognize the fact that the majority of us want more or less the same things, so we are actually on the same side even though we argue about how to get there. In business no one typically cares about how things get done so long as it all works. If we can be as open-minded and flexible in the world of politics, we will be able to solve or at least mitigate just about everything that ails our nation.

There are very possibly better ideas and suggestions than the ones laid out in this chapter, but it is hard to believe that the essential drivers of logic and business disciplines would not be beneficial. Who can imagine that politics would not be improved with increased doses of honesty, accountability, competition, customer focus, adaptability, efficiency, and measured effectiveness?

Chapter 11

Democracy 2.0

Have we left our democracy in the hands of politicians for too long —is there a new way?

As described earlier, the genius of the free market is that it thrives on human emotions but has built-in disciplines based on logic and truth that continuously push for success. Democracy has some of the same characteristics, and is one of the greatest human inventions, but it does not always recognize when change is necessary—and it does not consistently force timely reality checks. There is, therefore, a tendency for it to allow the misuse of societal resources which results in the nation becoming steadily poorer and less competitive.

The overall message of this book is that the only way to repair the corrupt, feckless, and outdated political system that we currently endure is to apply business-based disciplines to the running of our democracy. When that happens, the ensuing political environment will naturally become one that is based on competition, honesty, and competence—eventually resulting in an efficient and responsive government that naturally evolves to take on any future challenges.

Although we now have the motivation and the means, it would take quite the optimist to think that we could present radical changes to Congress and they would automatically implement them. There are many politicians and bureaucrats who will need to be pulled kicking and screaming into the 21st century. Why would they and their acolytes want to change? It's all quite comfortable for them and they would have to give up much of their unseen and discretionary power. But governments have been stirred into action before and maybe they can be again. A. C. Grayling, in his book *The Heart of Things*, gives us an example:

> *"London acquired a sewage system only when, one hot nineteenth-century summer, the Thames filth backed up all the way to Westminster, and its stench penetrated Parliament. An act was rapidly passed, at last reducing East End deaths from typhoid and dysentery."*

In other words, politicians need a bit of a push.

But how do we actually get things moving when there are so many interests vested in the status quo? There are many members of Congress fitting the stereotype of glad-handing party hacks who happily spout whatever can be made into a snappy sound bite and are ready to support anyone or anything that gets them prestige and votes. But let's not get too depressed. There are likely many other members who have become heartily fed up with the way politics has been going and have a genuine desire to work in the long-term best interests of the country—which is good, because we will need them if we are to move forward.

Getting Business Discipline Into Government

It is clear that we need some outside intervention and who better than industry leaders who have proven themselves to be successful in today's commercial environment? The right people would bring new ideas and the technical and managerial skills we so badly need. But just as importantly, they would bring strong leadership. When current or ex CEOs of world-renowned public companies put their name behind a project people will listen, and when people listen, politicians will likely follow suit.

The good news is that if we were to advertise for potential leaders to see the job through there would be plenty of qualified candidates. America is fortunate enough to have many genuinely self-made billionaires who have shown themselves to have what it takes to visualize opportunities and then manage the necessary business processes through all their various stages. And a number of these people are not just motivated by the acquisition of wealth. For example, Warren Buffet has encouraged a number of his fellow billionaires to make a pledge to donate more than half of their fortunes to philanthropic causes and some are prepared to donate their time and expertise.

Perhaps the best example of how qualified leadership can be applied to social issues is the way Bill and Melinda Gates set up and then actively manage a foundation dedicated to the proposition that "Everyone deserves a healthy and productive life". They have used expertise gained in the commercial world to alleviate and sometimes solve extremely complex problems that involve: politics, disease, education, poverty, logistics, money, and people from diverse cultural backgrounds. The Gates Foundation proved that it is possible to identify issues like specific diseases in far-off and poor developing countries and then cut mortality rates by 50% in 15 years. Bill Gates attributes much of the success of the foundation to the application of the same logic used at Microsoft, which was essentially the process of setting goals, planning, and then measuring progress. If it is possible to create a multi-billion-dollar business from nothing and eradicate a disease in foreign countries, surely we can adopt the lessons learned and apply them to the issue of governance in our own country.

Another example of an industry leader having the money, expertise, and will to make improvements in social welfare is Steve Balmer, the ex-CEO of Microsoft. He has bought into the concept of trying to make the government work more like a business and made the incredibly useful step of creating a source for all sorts of facts related to the running of government. This approach clearly follows one of the primary rules of business— base all decisions on the truth. A study of the website he created usafacts.org provides a wealth of information on the functioning of our government, including where the money comes from and where it goes.

Democracy Foundation

The proposal is that we attract industry leaders and get them to come together to create a team, or perhaps competing teams, to identify our real national priorities. But maybe we don't even have to wait for industry titans to step forward and self-finance all the operations. The establishment of teams funded by public donations through the internet is entirely consistent with the overall intent of the Foundation—providing they are demonstrably non-partisan and dedicated to the concept of developing proposals that address social issues in an efficient and verifiable manner. Regardless of the make-up of teams, their mission will be to establish realistic goals and then formulate data-supported plans that can then be published in a clear and understandable format. The electorate will then be able to understand the objectives and be assured that stated goals, costs, and time to implement are both realistic and can be monitored through to success. To avoid partisan games and ensure that the process is seen as fair and honest, politicians will not be involved until the final presentations are made. And it will be necessary to have a transparent code of ethics established so that there can be no hint of participants acting in a self-serving manner. Once the plans have been published, politicians will be invited to comment, support, and then sponsor the ones that they believe will benefit the nation. Once implemented, progress will be published on the internet at regular intervals so that the public can monitor progress and be assured that promises are being kept.

Regardless of exactly how the money is raised the following steps are proposed:

1. Create a foundation—let's call it the Democracy Foundation. Whether it is funded by business leaders or by crowd-funded donations teams will be formed which will be dedicated to the mission described earlier, which is:

   > *To enhance the performance of our democracy, thereby ensuring that America remains the most powerful nation on Earth, with*

equal opportunity and living standards that are at least equal to those of other wealthy nations.

2. Create a repository of unimpeachable data that describe facts relevant to public policy—in essence, the analysis of the performance of our society in significant areas. It will consist primarily of numbers that describe costs and outcomes, so that value can be assessed in such a manner that comparisons can be made, both domestically and internationally. The list must be restricted to facts and explanations, and be devoid of comment so that there cannot be accusations of political bias of any kind. It is intended that it be used as an accurate health-check of the nation and become the basis of establishing future national priorities.

3. Have the Democracy Foundation create a list of proposals that address performance issues that are having a significant impact on our quality of life and are a drain on our national resources thereby making us less competitive. The mandate should be as wide as possible and clearly include anything the government could do to improve our ability to advance the Mission. Most of the proposals will likely be related to the execution of well-recognized government activities, but should also include projects designed to improve competition in all areas of the economy including not only government operations but also the private sector. Addressing huge and far-reaching undertakings, like the improvement of productivity, should be encouraged. To avoid partisan attacks and confusion the proposals must be based on unimpeachable sources that cannot be realistically challenged.

There are many opportunities, but a few examples might include:

Competition - identify uncompetitive areas of the economy by analysis of pricing in all states and those in comparable foreign countries

<u>Health care</u>   - reduce costs as a percentage of GDP to the next highest in OECD
- reduce infant mortality and perinatal death to comparable OECD levels
- reduce maternal death to OECD levels

<u>Criminal Justice</u> - reduce crime rates without the cost and social damage caused by excessive rates of incarceration

<u>Infrastructure</u> - ensure all citizens have access to internet service with speed and pricing comparable to best performing European countries

<u>Education</u>   - reduce costs and improve performance
- develop a new education system that ensures students are prepared for the future
- develop programs to improve social mobility e.g., ensure all communities have equal education opportunities
- develop a continuing education system for adults that adapts to the changing needs of the economy

4.   Have the Democracy Foundation identify objectives, goals, and plans to address specific national issues that are both

significant and achievable. The process will be formulated along the lines of the powerful management process known as Objectives and Key Results (OKRs) as described in John Doerr's book *"Measuring What Matters"*. It is a process that has been used by many successful new companies starting with Intel and then being adopted by others including Adobe, Amazon, Dell, Microsoft, Netflix, Google, Facebook, etc. There really isn't anything magical about the process, it is just the personification of how organizations can harness blue-sky thinking and then make it happen by ensuring that well-established business disciplines are adhered to throughout the process.

5. Identify and enlist members of Congress who are prepared to give input and then sponsor specific goals for the purpose of enacting laws and taking responsibility for implementation. In doing so, members will be required to ensure sufficient resources and that the work is efficiently and effectively managed. They must also explain progress in monthly and quarterly reports and describe any necessary remedial action to be undertaken.

6. Have the Democracy Foundation develop a standardized data collection and reporting system such that progress towards every objective can be available for viewing by the general public on the their website.

Creating and maintaining the Democracy Foundation is the first step to ensuring that there is an overarching discipline based on keeping the focus on identifying essential needs and then managing issues through to resolution. But it can't stop there.

Chapter 12

The Fix:
Personal Responsibility

"One of the penalties for refusing to participate in politics is that you end up being governed by your inferiors"

— Plato

Our democracy was never intended to be a spectator sport. It requires the active participation of citizens who get involved and perform certain duties. The very least these being to show up on Election Day and vote. Clearly some put very much more effort than others into the political process. There are those who run for office, party members who volunteer, people who research issues and then vote and/or advocate, etc. The rest of us limit our involvement to voting for the party of our choice or the candidate that seems to offer something that is appealing at the time. And there are a bunch more who do not vote at all.

As described earlier, not many of us are truly happy with what is going on because we have gotten into a situation in which ideological agendas supported by sound bites carry more weight than solid solutions to real issues. It is clearly an unsatisfactory way of running our democracy and it prevents us from reaching our potential. The processes described earlier are intended to illustrate a pathway to creating a situation in which a clear-eyed analyses of important issues can be presented to the electorate— who will then be able to monitor progress in real time. It is expected that a new political culture will ensue, such that ideological pie-in-the-sky proposals with zero substance will no longer be tolerated and there will be an upsurge in innovative thinking driven by a genuine competition of workable ideas.

Of course, none of this will happen without the active involvement of the electorate—you and me. It is not simply a matter of waiting for someone else to put something in front of us so that we can then make a decision. We will have to do our homework, and that will involve doing something really hard because we have to work against some basic human impulses. The answer to not being emotionally manipulated is simple, but not easy. We have to call on our uniquely human ability to think logically by marshaling all available data and then making an appropriate decision.

Democracy vs Human Nature
As pointed out earlier, we have a problem. Evolution took the development of our brains to the point at which we were able to form functioning groups, each with its own social hierarchies and particular way of interacting, but then it stopped.

Skillful politicians have always been able to appeal to our emotions when looking for support. Appeals to our emotions can be a useful start to getting mobilized and getting things done. They certainly have their time and place—imminent attacks by enemies bent on destruction being one obvious example. But used gratuitously or for the wrong reasons they can become a useless diversion, or even make for a toxic environment. Because emotions are so powerful we should always be suspicious of politicians who make them front and center of their appeal.

Let's look at at just a few that are commonly used to whip up popular and urgent support:

> Insecurity   In its various forms has been the universal motivator since time began and for good reason. Threats to the safety of ourselves and family and the actual or impending loss of; income, food, shelter, social status, property, etc. produce a visceral reaction in humans which

leads to thoughts and behaviors that just would not have been imagined when life was comfortable and secure.

<u>Common Purpose</u> We were all born with an innate drive to gather with other people and work effectively to achieve a common goal, and it has been a major driver in human success. It pushes us to form groups, get the best out of individuals, and thereby bring about all sorts of advances that would otherwise be impossible. And we would much rather be part of effective groups, so we try to associate with others who demonstrate strength and success—the feelings of euphoria we get when our sports team wins is a clear demonstration of how much we like to identify ourselves as being part of successful groups. Although we enjoy success most sports fans are more loyal than might be expected. Some supporters stick with their team through long periods without any sign of success at all. Clearly there is an in-built human desire to join a winning team and thereby achieve a common goal, even through hard times. Because we have such a powerful desire to join in with something that looks like it will be successful, we lay ourselves open to an invitation to join even dubious causes particularly when we see others who we respect or admire getting involved. But we need to be careful—recruitment of young men at the beginning of wars has almost always been successful.

<u>Fairness</u> Since time began, it appears that one of the most powerful hard-wired traits in any human group has been a sense of fairness. Experiments have shown that the desire for fairness is common to all groups of people in every society in the world. The need for fairness is so strong that people will even give up rewards and ignore their own best interests if they feel they are being treated unfairly. They demand rules that judge their behaviors consistently and fairly, even though those rules might be difficult or even illogical. Because the desire for fairness runs so deep we are likely to be very interested in messages that indicate we are being cheated or taken advantage of in some way.

Racism   Although racism was once assumed to be a demonstration of the natural order it is now widely accepted to be morally wrong, socially destructive, and illogical, but it remains a potent emotion for a very good reason. The fear of different human beings is a protective mechanism which has been part of our make-up since before our hunter gatherer days. Imagine a tribe of early humans who have been living in a valley for years, maybe generations, and another human from the other side of the mountains shows up. His facial features, clothes, and language are all different. Without any information to the contrary, it is possible that this person represents a real danger because he might bring all manner of catastrophes. He might be violent, bring disease, and even more worryingly introduce new ideas that might corrupt society and bring about social decay. And you never know— cause all the game in the valley to disappear or prevent the sun from rising. Fear of different ethnicities is very similar to racism because people with different thoughts, ideas and behaviors could represent a threat until proven otherwise. It all sounds primitive and uninformed now, but we must remember our evolution more or less stopped thousands of years ago.

Strong Leader   Just about all social animals pick strong leaders, and we are no different. The reason stags with large antlers get to be the ones to breed is a simple matter of selecting the most powerful genes. Humans are somewhat more complex because the appearance of strength comes from more than physical attributes. Although it makes sense to pick a physically strong leader the ability to communicate ideas that influence people is also a demonstration of power. We are clearly drawn to strength, but sometimes what appears to be strength is actually neediness and a display of narcissism, or maybe an infatuation with the exercise of power.

Nationalism   Forming and then maintaining nations is really just an extension of the ancient desire to keep the tribe together and act for the benefit of all. As well as providing security it also engenders a feeling of identity and pride which can elevate performance when it comes to competing with other countries in terms of relative performance, such as athletics and commercial success. It is clearly an essential aspect of humanity and vital in times of war because it is necessary to come together and make sacrifices to protect a way of life that has been shown to be necessary for survival. Nationalism can have a dark side when it is used as a weapon to subjugate others, become a proxy for racism, or simply used as an easy way to garner political support.

Loyalty   We as a species have a built-in desire to be loyal to people close to us. So much so that being loyal is widely seen as being an admirable trait in a person's character. In difficult times such as famine, war, and even persecution of religion or ethnicity, the heightened impetus to stick together and share burdens has been an essential part of our ability to survive. The near death experiences of war exhibit some of the extreme examples of how loyalty can bring out the selfless side of our nature. Survivors of the WWII bombing of London talked of feeling a "Blitz Spirit" of togetherness that was not experienced before or since. And soldiers of many wars have talked of the feeling of comradeship that survived enemy attacks and even the inept leadership of their own officers. But being unquestioningly loyal can be something of a double-edged sword. It is an emotion that has served us well through many troubled times, but it can have an unproductive and possibly dangerous side. Once we are on board with the feeling of being "on the team" we often find it difficult to let go, even when there is clear evidence that our continued loyalty makes no sense.

Learned Experiences   At the moment of conception our inherited genes set about preprogramming our brains in such a way that much of our basic behavioral characteristics are in place before we are born. Although we are born with innate abilities and even predispositions that is not the end of the story by any means. Much of our early life is spent trying to make sense of the world—much of it basic and practical like recognizing what is dangerous, tastes bad, etc., but a great deal of effort goes into interpreting patterns of behavior in other humans. By the time we reach adulthood we are a complex mix of nature and nurture with many of our fundamental attitudes set in place by our own unique experience and education. Apart from some notable formative experiences we often do not know why we think the way we do, but we do know that we are right. The trouble is that once we have seen, learned, and accepted something it then becomes our "truth." Mark Twain was an astute observer of human nature and is reputed to have said:

"It is easier to fool people than it is to convince them that they have been fooled"

Maybe the use of the word "fool" could be taken as somewhat pejorative—we could easily substitute the word "mislead" and the gist of the quotation would be the same. We might be right or wrong, but it does not matter. The last thing we want to do is change our fundamental beliefs.

<u>Social Status</u> Predictable interactions with others is an essential element of societies throughout the animal kingdom. As described in Chapter 1. dogs inherited the motivation to fit into a hierarchy and that is one of the reasons that they blend successfully with human families. But things do not always go well. If a dog is not trained properly, it can sometimes get confused and start acting up simply because they don't know who the leader is and where they stand relative to other members of the "pack". We humans are not that different—some of us have a desire to take up the challenge to be the leader, but that isn't for everyone. Most people are happy to fill a position that requires them follow the leader, but exercise some authority over others.

Still more readily fit into a position in which they act along with their peers, getting respect and taking instructions from above whilst cooperating with others who are on the same level. That all sounds well and good and so long as nothing changes—it is a recipe for a peaceful coexistence— accommodating a few minor adjustments up and down, so long as nothing too drastic happens. It does, however, get serious when someone's social status is fundamentally challenged such that they lose power and prestige, or simply feel that they don't get the respect they deserve. That seems obvious for those with powerful positions, but it is also true for those on the lower rungs of the influence ladder. Absolutely no one likes to be pushed down to a lower level, and it is always possible to go down. The feeling that a person gets when they are rendered less useful and consequently command less respect is gut wrenching. Appealing to those who feel unfairly abused is, therefore, fertile ground for politicians who see an opportunity to convince people that the reason they are suffering is not their fault, but caused by forces outside their control and possibly a system that is rigged against them.

Recognizing the fact that our approach to coexisting with other members of our pack was largely mapped out in the brains of our pre-human forebears who competed with wolves for food should give us pause when we think about how we go about running our democracy. Can the emotions that drive social behavior set in place to ensure the survival of hunter-gatherer groups really be consistent with a sophisticated democracy, particularly when they make us susceptible to skillfully crafted political messaging? The answer is a qualified yes. If we are to do so we will have to break the habit of <u>reacting</u> like humans and reinforce our capability of <u>thinking</u> like humans. We can obviously keep bumbling along in our current sub-optimal fashion, but if we want to raise our game and get closer to achieving our full potential we will have to recognize when we are relying on our deep-seated human emotions. And that is not always easy. As pointed out in earlier chapters, emotion has always played a big part of politics, as it should. We are social animals and we need an emotional impetus to get motivated. Just as importantly, emotions drive all of our innermost drives to be good citizens, such as: our sense of fair play, morality and empathy. But basing decisions on emotions alone will never be the most efficient and effective way to run all aspects of a big and diverse country. After we feel the emotion we must test the concept with logic.

Taking Control

Consistent with the overall theme of imposing everyday commercial free market disciplines to our political processes it is suggested that we play the part of a knowledgeable customer. In particular a corporate purchaser rather than retail customer. The reason being that retail customers are only concerned with themselves and immediate family so they have a perfect right to buy anything on offer, however frivolous, so long as they can afford it. The responsibilities of corporate purchasers are different because the quality of their decisions affect their employers' ability to operate efficiently and thereby offer products of value to their own customers. That seems to be a good analogy because when we "buy" what a politician is selling we are accepting their promises on behalf of the nation, just as the corporate purchaser takes responsibility for goods and services that the company is to use.

There are a number ways corporate purchasers start the ball rolling when the company wishes to place a significant contract for goods and services. One way is to send out for expressions of interest that typically define performance requirements, and then select a qualified proponent that is believed to be capable of delivering what is required at an acceptable price.

This method will be applied to our political process if we play an active part in converting our democracy to the data and results-driven model outlined in Chapter 10, if we:

1. Understand that your reaction to political messaging and proposals will be affected by our own personal intuitive ethics, but be skeptical. Ask if the proposal represents a plan to benefit the nation or if it has been crafted to tell me what I want to hear.

2. Do not look for malign motivations, the guilty, or enemies —it is most likely that we are just having to deal with people with different opinions and ideas regarding how to proceed. Put emotions to one side and use logic to look for common ground in terms of desired outcomes.

3. Look for boring and mundane rather than flashy and exciting—it is more likely to represent good governance. For example: keeping maintenance up to date, management of public assets, and accurate public-sector accounting can all lead to improvements in the allocation of resources.

4. Support the Democracy Foundation so that politicians understand there is a groundswell of support for the concept of fact-based and performance-driven government. The Foundation might use polling companies to understand the public's priorities and then produce the equivalent of expressions of interest which can then be tested to see if there is public support. On the basis of feedback the Democracy Foundation can then craft a number of Policy Objectives each with its own defined measurable interim goals, together with supporting documentation.

5. Insist that our political representatives study and stake out their position on Policy Objectives. If they choose rejection we must ensure that they produce their own competing objectives with equivalent supporting documentation.

6. Encourage members of Congress from both sides to sponsor and then shepherd Policy Objectives right through to continued successful implementation. Follow progress and

demand corrective action if it appears that the program is not on track to meet its schedule or defined ultimate objectives.

Above all else, and as noted earlier, be particularly suspicious of politicians who base their appeal on emotions. The following is a list of emotions and examples of political messages that are intended to evoke them:

- Fear plays to our basic human need to react to insecurity of all kinds. Although there can be real circumstances warranting immediate and strong action, constant and loud protestations should be treated with suspicion.

  "There are many things out there that will hurt you and family unless you vote for me".

- Patriotism is a good and productive human trait that has helped drive progress through active competition between nations, but taken to an extreme it can become just an easy political substitute for thoughtful consideration and remedies for real issues.

  "Our country is the best in the world and we deserve to always be on top. Only I can make sure our country regains its strength and standing in the world"

- Ethnicity and race can be used to appeal to our innate feelings of tribalism because it is based on the ancient fear that unless proven otherwise strangers can be a danger. It is a very powerful message, particularly to those who feel dispossessed in some way.

  "You need someone to stand up for people like you and the culture you were raised in"

- Blame everything that goes wrong is someone else's fault.

"It is my mission to help you because all those other people are making it impossible for you to rise to the potential you deserve. The problem is them—you don't have to change"

- Victimization is a powerful message, because hearing that all your problems are the result of others taking advantage of you can feel comfortable, particularly if you are not doing that well.

"Your situation is not your fault. People with power and influence are taking advantage of you and keeping you down"

- Blue-sky promises are nice to hear because everyone wants things to go better. So unsubstantiated claims of a better future are standard fare in the world of politics. We currently have a political culture that lacks the discipline of consequences, so we continue to be misled and just assume that politicians cannot be trusted.

"I will cut costs, build infrastructure, spend more on defense, lower taxes, give you better service and reduce the deficit—and no one will feel any pain.

- Loyalty to our group and people like us is a strong emotion because we humans have always been more comfortable when we feel as though we belong to a group and will very often set aside our own personal interests for those we identify with. When faced with a cultural question, we intuitively give an answer based on what we perceive the rest of our team thinks. Like so many aspects of human nature, our propensity for groupthink has been a major factor in our success as a species, but if it is not brought into question every now and then everyone will fall off the cliff at the same time.

"If we stick together we can protect each other, and we have to, because we are being attacked"

- Altruism and empathy are a natural human feelings and they are the impetus for people to help others who are suffering in some way. Aiding people with difficulties is clearly a demonstration of a society's better side and a mark of civilization. But there is a downside, particularly when it goes too far. If the process is too generous it can bring about an inefficient reallocation of national resources—and personal responsibility can take a back seat to apathy and even feelings of resentment and entitlement.

"The wealthy can afford to pay more, and if you don't support this social program you obviously don't care about people"

Being skeptical of our own emotions is not easy because our intuitive ethics are always the first port of call in our brains. We have to continuously keep reminding ourselves that our first reaction is not necessarily the product of logical thought. We should be particularly suspicious of our own initial reactions if our choice of news outlets and friends invariably agree with our own point of view.

We owe it to ourselves and our country to get out of our comfort zone and re-examine why we react the way we do, then search out facts supported by data, and:

Be Informed - Vote Wisely - Stay Involved

Appendix

Opportunities

The process of making purchases is a part of our daily lives, and to a lesser or greater extent we choose to buy on the basis of value. When we pay more for the extra comfort and service that an upmarket hotel offers we do so because we have made the judgement that it is worth the extra expenditure. We make these kinds of decisions for many items we buy on a daily basis, and by and large it is a very efficient mechanism for providing items that suit everyone's needs at a price they can afford.

There are, however, huge portions of our monthly expenditures that are not subject to any decisions we might make with regard to judging value. In general, these are the basic services described in earlier chapters that can be provided by the government directly or companies subject to government control and/or in receipt of subsidies. As a nation, we clearly have to pay for basic services, but how do we know we are getting value? One way or another we have to find out—one way might be to see how efficiently we provide services compared to other nations that are our commercial competitors.

The following are just a few examples of some issues that could easily be identified as areas of opportunity for creating measurable objectives to both: reduce our national overhead and thereby become more competitive, and improve our overall quality of life.

1. **Free and Fair Competition:** As described earlier, the fundamental pillars of our society, democracy and free market capitalism are mutually dependent and both need to

be nurtured if we are to prosper and remain free. All areas of the economy should be investigated to discover and correct situations in which there is evidence of a lack of competition. Excessive profits are but one example—others include: wage suppression, lack of choice, higher than international pricing, unnecessary permitting/licensing, and restrictive non-compete employment contracts.

2. **Healthcare**: We spend $10,224 per person/year, which is much more than the $5,280 average of nine comparably wealthy countries. Those countries have similar prescription drug usage, but they manage to keep their average yearly cost down to roughly half our yearly per person cost of $1,000. For all the additional cost, you would expect our results to be better than our competitors but they are not. These countries all have greater life expectancies and our infant mortality rate of 5.8 per 100,000 is much worse than the 3.4 per 100,000 average achieved by comparable countries. We do, however, look good when it comes to wait times to see specialists and have elective surgery, but even there we are not the best compared to less costly comparable countries.

3. **Criminal Justice**: America incarcerates more of our citizens than other country. Our nation represents 5% of the world's population, but we hold 25% of all prisoners. Comparable countries have found much more cost effective ways to punish and rehabilitate their criminals, thereby avoiding the obvious direct and consequential costs of taking people out of the workforce and then reducing the likelihood of employment upon release.

4. **Broadband**: We all know how much our lives are affected by the digital economy and a report produced by the World Bank in 2009 underlined just how important access is to each and every nation. The report stated that there is a 1.38% increase in GDP for every 10% increase in broadband penetration. We do have pretty good penetration, but it is disappointing to see that we are not world leaders in the use

of this essential technology. The combination of value and performance is illustrated by the fact that we rank 10th in terms of speed and among the worst in the developed world when it comes to cost. Value for money is not great either—we rank 42nd in the world in terms of "bang for the buck."

5. **College Tuition:** We are all very aware of the fact that the cost of college tuition has risen at an alarming rate for the last several years, and it does not look like there will be a slow down in the near future. Tuition cost has more than doubled since the 1980s and the total amount of student debt is now estimated to be approximately $1.5 trillion.

    The suggested reasons are many and varied: faculties are overpaid, students have easy access to loans, prices are set by wealthy students who do not even require loans, state support has been reduced, expensive facilities and services have been added, more students want a college education—the list of potential culprits goes on.

    Regardless of cause the effect of excessively high college education it is obviously felt mostly by young people starting off on their careers, which has at least two big effects. Firstly, it is easy to imagine that this younger generation will feel that society has not treated them as fairly as their parents' generation who were able to gain relatively well paid and secure jobs without ruinous college loans. It has the appearance of a society happy to ensure the well-being of taxpayers, financial institutions and educational elites at their expense. Secondly, because graduates are spending money repaying loans they are less able to purchase discretionary items there is a detrimental impact to the overall economy.

6. **Tough Issues:** The fact that people have made their minds up about the rights and wrongs of issues on the basis of deeply held views must not preclude the search for information and the presentation of relevant facts. If we accept the proposition that we will all be better served by

developing a data-driven and results-based society there will be no issues exempt from informed discussion, including: cyber security, wealth disparity, opioid epidemic, immigration, climate change, and gun violence, etc., etc.

These are just a few possible areas of opportunity for improvement in the provision of basic services largely brought about by the government abrogating its responsibilities and not keeping up with the times. With everything in life changing so quickly, politicians have been unable to come up with workable ideas to address the real problems. They have stuck to their outdated guns, and deadlock has been the result. The effects of which should be shocking to every American brought up believing that this country leads the world in just about everything. Michael Porter, a professor at the Harvard Business School, has produced some incredibly detailed, but easily understood, data in what is called the "Social Progress Index" (www.socialprogress.org) The index measures the leading indicators of social progress and groups them into three basic categories:

> **Basic Human Needs**: nutrition and basic medical care, water and sanitation, shelter, personal safety
> **Foundations of Well Being**: access to basic knowledge, access to information and communications, health and wellness, ecosystem sustainability.
> **Opportunity**: personal rights, personal freedom and choice, tolerance and inclusion, access to advanced education

Health care performance drags America's index down, but that is well understood. What does come as a surprise is America's relatively poor performance in other areas, such as access to information, opportunity, and personal rights. What is so useful about this index is that it is based on facts and outcomes, not political messages and how much money is spent. It can, therefore, be used to establish goals and strategies to efficiently achieve best-in-class performance.

As described earlier, there has been a failure to recognize common goals because too much time is spent arguing matters of entrenched political principle. For example, because arguments tend to focus on the amount of money the government spends, there is apparently no obvious way to differentiate between money to be spent on maintaining services and investments that might reduce long-term costs for society. Quite simply, there needs to be a way to force the issue of value into the political arena.

But the situation is not hopeless. In fact, there are many reasons to feel optimistic. We have a long history of doing what it takes once we recognize problems, and we currently have the mechanisms to tackle any of today's challenges. First and foremost, we have well-run strong businesses operated by an energetic and innovative workforce. But those businesses could do even better if we remove the yoke of poorly identified priorities and inefficiently managed basic services. Once we recognize that applying well understood basic business principles we will inevitably become a more democratic, healthier, and more competitive nation.

All the ideas and suggestions contained in this book are not intended to be the final word. Feedback, whether it be supportive, or of a challenging nature, would be be greatly appreciated.

Please contact the author at:
savingourdemocracycm@gmail.com

Notes

Introduction

Rachel Foster. Healthcare in Canada vs USA: Facing High Costs or Long Wait Times, healthcare.com, https://www.healthcare.com/blog/canada-vs-usa-healthcare/, November 30, 2018.

Chapter 1: What My Dog Taught Me

1. "U.S. Pet Ownership Statistics". *Pet Ownership and Demographics Sourcebook*. https://www.avma.org/KB/Resources/Statistics/Pages/Market-research-statistics-US-pet-ownership.aspx. 2012.

2. Mary Bates. "Prehistoric Puppy May be Earliest Evidence of Pet-Human Bonding." *National Geographic*. https://news.nationalgeographic.com/2018/02/ancient-pet-puppy-oberkassel-stone-age-dog/. February 27, 2018.

3. Chuck Jones. "Trump's Economic Scorecard: 18 months into his presidency." *Forbes*. https://www.forbes.com/sites/chuckjones/2018/07/27/trumps-economic-scorecard-18-months-into-his-presidency/#55c572b1283e. July 27, 2018

4. "Map of Human Migration." *National Geographic*. https://genographic.nationalgeographic.com/human-journey/. December 11, 2018.

5. "Climate Effects on Human Evolution." *Smithsonian National Museum of Natural History*. http://humanorigins.si.edu/research/climate-and-human-evolution/climate-effects-human-evolution. December 10, 2018.

6. Vaudeville Reddy. "Getting back to the rough ground: Deception and social living." *The Royal Society B Biological Sciences*.

https://www.researchgate.net/publication/6495566_Getting_back_to_the_rough_ground_Deception_and_'social_living'. April 2007.

7. C. Moon, H. Lagercrantz, P.K. Kulac. "Language Experienced in utero affects vowel perception after birth." *Acta Pediatrica.* https://onlinelibrary.wiley.com/doi/abs/10.1111/apa.12098. December 20, 2018.

8. Johnathon Haidt. "The Righteous Mind." *Vantage Books.* 2012.

Chapter 5: Where Are We?

1. Laurence Michel. Elise Gould, Josh Bidens. "Wage Stagnation in Nine Charts." *Economic Policy Institute.* https://www.epi.org/publication/charting-wage-stagnation/. January 6, 2015.

2. Ana Gonzalez-Barrera and Jens Manuel Krogstad. "What we know about illegal immigration from Mexico." *Pew Research Center.* http://www.pewresearch.org/topics/unauthorized-immigration/2017/. Mar 2, 2017.

3. D'Vera Cohn, Jeffrey S. Passel, and Ana Gonzalez-Barrera. "Rise in US Immigrants from El Salvador, Guatemala, and Honduras Outpaces Growth from Elsewhere." *Pew Research Center.* http://www.pewhispanic.org/2017/12/07/rise-in-u-s-immigrants-from-el-salvador-guatemala-and-honduras-outpaces-growth-from-elsewhere/. December 2017.

3. Gilliam H. Frey. "US White population declines and Generation "Z Plus" is minority White, census shows." *Brookings Institution.* https://www.brookings.edu/blog/the-avenue/2018/06/21/us-white-population-declines-and-generation-z-plus-is-minority-white-census-shows/. June 22, 2018.

4. "Mortality in the United States: Past Present, and Future." *Penn Wharton University of Pennsylvania* . http://

budgetmodel.wharton.upenn.edu/issues/2016/1/25/mortality-in-the-united-states-past-present-and-future. 2013.

5. "Crime in the U.S., 1960-2017." *Uniform Crime Reporting Program.* http://www.disastercenter.com/crime/uscrime.htm. 2017.

6. Barry Latzer. "Do Hard Times spark more crime?" *LA Times.* https://www.latimes.com/opinion/op-ed/la-oe-latzer-crime-economy-20140124-story.html. 2014.

7. "The US Continues to be One of the Least Taxed of the Developed Countries." *Citizens for Tax Justice (OECD is source).* https://www.ctj.org/the-u-s-continues-to-be-one-of-the-least-taxed-of-the-developed-countries/. 2013.

Chapter 6: Government: Costs and Effects

1. Definition citation *Overhead.* https://www.dictionary.com/browse/overhead.

2. Bradley Sawyer and Cynthia Cox. "How does Healthcare Spending in the US compare to other countries?" *Peterson Kaiser.* https://www.healthsystemtracker.org/chart-collection/health-spending-u-s-compare-countries/. 2016.

3. Brooks Jackson. "The Budget and Deficit Under Clintons." Fact check.org,https://www.factcheck.org/2008/02/the-budget-and-deficit-under-clinton/, 2008.

4. Christopher Chantrill. "US National debt and and Deficit History,." *USGOVERNMENTSPENDING.ORG.* https://www.usgovernmentspending.com/debt_deficit_history. 2018.

5. "Average electricity prices Around the World." *OVO Energy.* https://www.ovoenergy.com/guides/energy-guides/average-electricity-prices-kwh.html. 2018.

6. "America's big spending on health Care doesn't pay off." *The Economist*. https://www.economist.com/united-states/2015/11/16/americas-big-spending-on-health-care-doesnt-pay-off. 2015.

7. Lisa Rapaport. "U.S. health spending twice other countries' with worse results." *Reuters*. https://www.reuters.com/article/us-health-spending/u-s-health-spending-twice-other-countries-with-worse-results-idUSKCN1GP2YN. 2018.

8. David Mulhausen. "Evaluating Federal Social Programs." *Heritage Foundation*. https://www.heritage.org/government-regulation/report/evaluating-federal-social-programs-finding-out-what-works-and-what. July 2011.

9. "Wisconsin is Twice as Likely to Imprison People as Minnesota." *The Economist*. https://www.economist.com/united-states/2018/10/20/wisconsin-is-twice-as-likely-to-imprison-people-as-minnesota. October 20, 2018.

10. "The Moral Failures of America's Prison-Industrial Complex." *The Economist*. https://www.economist.com/democracy-in-america/2015/07/20/the-moral-failures-of-americas-prison-industrial-complex. July 20, 2015.

11. "The Growth of Incarceration on the United States." *National Academics Press*. https://www.nap.edu/catalog/18613/the-growth-of-incarceration-in-the-united-states-exploring-causes. 2014.

12. Lindsey Devers. "Plea Charge and Bargaining, Bureau of Justice Assistance." https://www.bja.gov/Publications/PleaBargainingResearchSummary.pdf. January 24, 2011.

13. Michael Toury. "Why Crime Rates are Falling Throughout the Western World." *University of Minnesota Law School*. https://scholarship.law.umn.edu/faculty_articles/511/. 2014.

14. Michael Ye Hee Lee. "Yes, U.S. locks People up at a higher rate than other countries", *Washington Post.* https://www.washingtonpost.com/news/fact-checker/wp/2015/07/07/yes-u-s-locks-people-up-at-a-higher-rate-than-any-other-country/?utm_term=.6ce6a565f1be. July 7, 2015.

15. "Highest to Lowest - Prison Population Rate." *Birkbeck, University of London. World Prison Brief.* http://www.prisonstudies.org/highest-to-lowest/prison-population-total.

16. Neil Schoenherr. "Cost of Incarceration in the U.S. More than \$1 trillion." *Washington University in St. Louis.* https://source.wustl.edu/2016/09/cost-incarceration-u-s-1-trillion/. October 7, 2016.

17. John Gramlich. "The Gap between the Blacks and Whites in Prison is Shrinking." *Pew Research Center.* http://www.pewresearch.org/fact-tank/2018/01/12/shrinking-gap-between-number-of-blacks-and-whites-in-prison/. January 13, 2018.

18. Linda Young. "High-Achieving Black Women and Marriage." *Psychology Today.* https://www.psychologytoday.com/ca/blog/love-in-limbo/201006/high-achieving-black-women-and-marriage-not-choosing-or-not-chosen. June 14, 2010.

19. "Kaiser Health Tracking Poll: November 2016." *Henry J. Kaiser Family Foundation.* https://www.kff.org/health-costs/poll-finding/kaiser-health-tracking-poll-november-2016/. December 1, 2018.

20. Bradley Sawyer and Cynthia Cox. "How has U.S. spending on health care changed over time." *Henry J. Kaiser Family Foundation.* https://www.healthsystemtracker.org/chart-collection/u-s-spending-healthcare-changed-time/. 2018.

21. "2016 Annual Report." *United Health Foundation.* https://www.americashealthrankings.org/learn/reports/2016-annual-report. 2016.

22. Eric Schneider MD, Dani O. Sarnak, David Squires, Arnav Shah, Michelle M. Doty. "Mirror, mirror 2017: International Comparison reflects Flaws and Opportunities for Better U.S. Healthcare." *The Commonwealth Fund.* https://www.commonwealthfund.org/publications/fund-reports/2017/jul/mirror-mirror-2017-international-comparison-reflects-flaws-and. July 2017.

23. Walter Frick. "Big Companies Don't Pat as Well as They used to." *Harvard Business Review.* https://hbr.org/2017/02/big-companies-dont-pay-as-well-as-they-used-to. February 13, 2017.

Chapter 7: Government: Can We Do Better?

1. Need Burton. "Plato on Democracy, Tyranny, and the Ideal State." *Psychology Today.* https://www.psychologytoday.com/ca/blog/hide-and-seek/201607/plato-democracy-tyranny-and-the-ideal-state. 2016.

2. Arash Abizadeh. "The Passions of the Wise:Rhetoric, and Aristotle's Passionate Practical Deliberation." academia.edu, https://www.jstor.org/stable/20131817?seq=1#page_scan_tab_contents. 2002.

Chapter 8: What Are Our Choices?

1. Robert Greenstein, Richard Kogan, and Roderick Taylor. "Program Spending Outside Social Security and Medicare Historically Low as a Percent of GDP and Projected to Fall Even Further." *Center on Budget and Policy Priorities.* https://www.cbpp.org/research/federal-budget/program-spending-outside-social-security-and-medicare-historically-low-as-a. 2018.

2. "Policy Basics: Top Ten Facts about Social Security" *Center on Budget and Policy Priorities.* https://www.cbpp.org/research/social-security/policy-basics-top-ten-facts-about-social-security

Chapter 10: Evolving Government

1. RJ Reinhart. "Republicans More Positive on U.S. Relations With Russia." *Gallup.* https://news.gallup.com/poll/237137/republicans-positive-relations-russia.aspx. July 12, 2017.

Appendix

1. "Large gains can come from mundane improvements in policy." *The Economist.* https://www.economist.com/leaders/2018/10/20/large-economic-gains-can-come-from-mundane-improvements-in-policy. October 20, 2018.

2. Bradley Sawyer, Cynthia Cox. "How doe health Spending in the U.S. Compare to Other Countries?" *Peterson-Kaiser Health Tracker.* https://www.healthsystemtracker.org/chart-collection/health-spending-u-s-compare-countries/. December 7, 2018.

3. "Life Expectancy at Birth." *CIA World Fact Book.* https://www.cia.gov/library/publications/the-world-factbook/rankorder/2102rank.html. 2018.

4. Dana O. Sana'a, David Squires, Shawn Bishop. "Paying for Prescription Drugs Around the World: Why is U.S. an Outlier." *Commonwealth Fund.* https://www.commonwealthfund.org/publications/issue-briefs/2017/oct/paying-prescription-drugs-around-world-why-us-outlier. October 5, 2017

5. Bradley Sawyer, Selena Gonzales. "How Does Infant Mortality Compare With Other Countries?" *Peterson-Kaiser Health Tracker.* https://www.healthsystemtracker.org/chart-collection/infant-mortality-u-s-compare-countries/. July 10, 2017.

6. Michelle Ye Hee Lee. "Yes, the U.S. locks People Up at a Higher Rate Than Other Countries." *Washington Post.* https://www.washingtonpost.com/news/fact-checker/wp/2015/07/07/yes-u-s-locks-people-up-at-a-higher-rate-than-any-other-country/?utm_term=.d97bb58462a7. July 7, 2015.

7. "International Comparison Requirements Pursuant to the Broadband Data Improvement Act GN Docket No. 17-199." *Federal Communications Commission, International Comparison Requirements Pursuant to the Broadband Data Improvement Act GN Docket No. 17-199.* February 2, 2018.

8. Mike Hanlon. "Broadband bang per buck:How your country rates on speed versus cost." *New atlas.com/author/mike-hanlon (cable.co.uk).* https://newatlas.com/broadband-speed-versus-cost-country-comparison/52346/. November 27, 2017

9. Hillary Hoffower. "College is more expensive than it's ever been, and 5 reasons why suggest it's only going to get worse". *Business Insider.* https://www.businessinsider.com/why-is-college-so-expensive-2018-4. July 8, 2018

10. NJ Lichnir. "The real reasons why college tuition is so high and what you can do about it". *The Scholarship System.* https://thescholarshipsystem.com/blog-for-students-families/the-real-reasons-why-college-tuition-is-so-high-and-what-you-can-do-about-it/. February 24, 2019